D1062043

02/2

STAND PRICE
$ 5.00

WILLIAM SHAKESPEARE:
THE TAMING OF THE SHREW

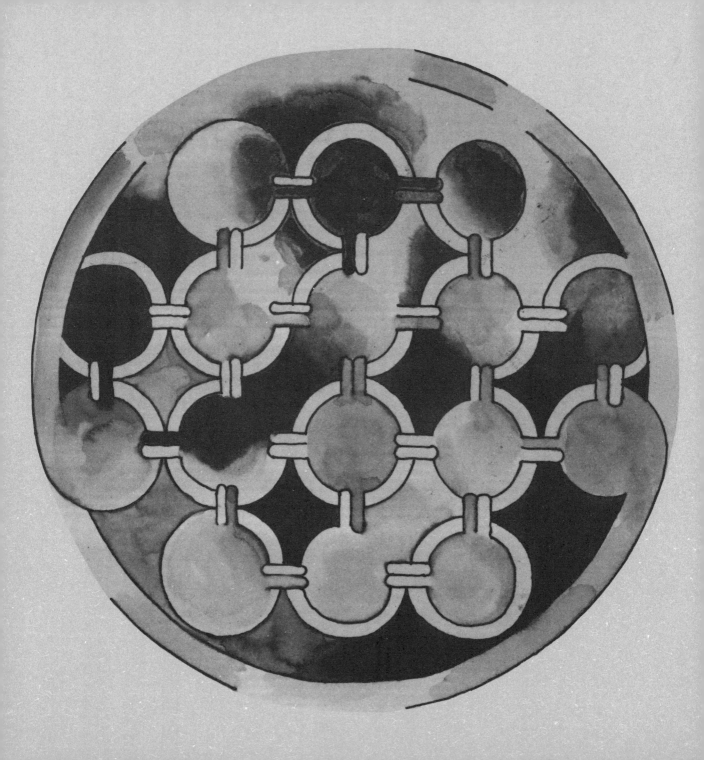

THE TAMING OF

THE SHREW

By WILLIAM SHAKESPEARE

DESIGN BY DANIEL HABERMAN
ILLUSTRATIONS BY ISADORE SELTZER

PUBLISHED BY
THE COMPOSING ROOM, INC.
THOMPSON LITHOGRAPHIC ASSOCIATES INC.
FINCH, PRUYN & COMPANY, INC.

COPYRIGHT © 1973 THE COMPOSING ROOM INC., NEW YORK CITY

INTRODUCTION—*An equivocal farce*

The Taming of the Shrew, by William Shakespeare,
is the seventh in a series of annual keepsakes prepared for the
friends of the publishers.

Completed in 1594, there is general disagreement as to the source as
well as the meaning of this early farce. While we can hardly
know what the youthful poet was thinking, we do know that Shakespeare
was enjoying the use of *double entendre* in other early plays such as
Love's Labor's Lost, Two Gentlemen of Verona, etcetera.

One can conveniently read different meanings into the play to conform to one's
bias: Is Kate tamed? Or is she the tamer? Is Kate truly the shrew?
Or is Bianca? If the farce is a prelude to *Much Ado About Nothing,*
is it not also the precursor to James Barrie's, *What Every Woman Knows?*
Perhaps Sir Philip Sidney's comment is most appropriate: "Comedy
is an imitation of the common errors of our life".
The first Folio edition of 1623 was used as a guide in the preparation of this
book. The publishers are indebted to Isadore Seltzer, whose illustrations
reflect sensitive attention to the characters in the play, and
whose time was generously given.

Warwick; Padua; and near Verona.

DRAMATIS PERSONAE

CHRISTOPHER SLY, *a tinker*

HOSTESS, *of an alehouse*

A LORD, *passing through*

BARTHOLOMEW, *a page*

BAPTISTA MINOLA, *father to Kate and Bianca*

KATE, *the shrew*

BIANCA, *sister to Kate*

PETRUCHIO, *suitor to Kate*

LUCENTIO, *(Cambia) suitor to Bianca*

GREMIO, *suitor to Bianca*

HORTENSIO, *(Litio) suitor to Bianca*

VINCENTIO, *father to Lucentio*

A PEDANT, *impersonating Vincentio*

TRANIO, *later impersonating Lucentio*

BIONDELLO, *servant to Lucentio*

GRUMIO, *servant to Petruchio*

WIDOW, HUNTSMEN, PLAYERS, OTHERS

INDUCTION

SCENE I

OUTSIDE RURAL ALEHOUSE

[Enter Hostess and Beggar, Christopher Sly]

Sly.   I'll pheeze you, in faith.

Hostess.   A pair of stocks, you rogue!

Sly.   Y'are a baggage, the Slys are no rogues. Look in the chronicles; we came in with Richard Conqueror. Therefore, *paucas pallabris;* let the world slide. Sessa!

Hostess.   You will not pay for the glasses you have burst?

Sly.   No, not a denier. Go, by St. Jeronimy, go to thy cold bed and warm thee.

Hostess.   I know my remedy: I must go fetch the thirdborough.
     [Exit]

Sly.   Third or fourth or fifth borough, I'll answer him by law. I'll not budge an inch, boy; let him come and kindly.
     [Falls asleep]

[Wind horns. Enter a Lord
from hunting, with his train]

Lord. Huntsman, I charge thee, tender well my hounds.
Broach Merriman—the poor cur is embossed—
And couple Clowder with the deep-mouthed brach.
Saw'st thou not, boy, how Silver made it good
At the hedge-corner in the coldest fault?
I would not lose the dog for twenty pound.

First Huntsman. Why, Bellman is as good as he, my lord;
He cried upon it at the merest loss
And twice today picked out the dullest scent.
Trust me, I take him for the better dog.

Lord. Thou art a fool. If Echo were as fleet,
I would esteem him worth a dozen such.
But sup them well and look unto them all.
Tomorrow I intend to hunt again.

First Huntsman. I will, my lord.

Lord.	What's here? One dead or drunk? See, doth he breathe?
Second Huntsman.	He breathes, my lord. Were he not warmed with ale,
	This were a bed but cold to sleep so soundly.
Lord.	O monstrous beast, how like a swine he lies!
	Grim death, how foul and loathsome is thine image!
	Sirs, I will practice on this drunken man.
	What think you, if he were conveyed to bed,
	Wrapped in sweet clothes, rings put upon his fingers,
	A most delicious banquet by his bed,
	And brave attendants near him when he wakes—
	Would not the beggar then forget himself?
First Huntsman.	Believe me, lord, I think he cannot choose.
Second Huntsman.	It would seem strange unto him when he waked.
Lord.	Even as a flatt'ring dream or worthless fancy.
	Then take him up and manage well the jest.
	Carry him gently to my fairest chamber
	And hang it round with all my wanton pictures;
	Balm his foul head in warm distillèd waters

And burn sweet wood to make the lodging sweet.
Procure me music ready when he wakes
To make a dulcet and a heavenly sound;
And if he chance to speak, be ready straight
And with a low submissive reverence
Say, "What is it your honor will command?"
Let one attend him with a silver basin
Full of rose water and bestrewed with flowers;
Another bear the ewer, the third a diaper,
And say, "Will't please your lordship cool your hands?"
Some one be ready with a costly suit
And ask him what apparel he will wear,
Another tell him of his hounds and horse
And that his lady mourns at his disease.
Persuade him that he hath been lunatic,
And when he says he is, say that he dreams,
For he is nothing but a mighty lord.
This do, and do it kindly, gentle sirs.
It will be pastime passing excellent
If it be husbanded with modesty.

First Huntsman. My lord, I warrant you we will play our part

As he shall think by our true diligence

He is no less than what we say he is.

Lord. Take him up gently and to bed with him,

And each one to his office when he wakes.

[*Sly is carried out. Sound trumpets*]

Sirrah, go see what trumpet 'tis that sounds.

[*Exit Servingman*]

Belike some noble gentleman that means,

Traveling some journey, to repose him here.

[*Enter Servingman*]

How now? Who is it?

Servingman. An't please your honor, players

That offer service to your lordship.

[*Enter Players*]

Lord. Bid them come near.

Now, fellows, you are welcome.

Players. We thank your honor.

Lord. Do you intend to stay with me tonight?

A Player.	So please your lordship to accept our duty.
Lord.	With all my heart. This fellow I remember
	Since once he played a farmer's eldest son;
	'Twas where you wooed the gentlewoman so well.
	I have forgot your name, but sure that part
	Was aptly fitted and naturally performed.
Second Player.	I think 'twas Soto that your honor means.
Lord.	'Tis very true; thou didst it excellent.
	Well, you are come to me in happy time,
	The rather for I have some sport in hand
	Wherein your cunning can assist me much.
	There is a lord will hear you play tonight.
	But I am doubtful of your modesties,
	Lest over-eyeing of his odd behavior—
	For yet his honor never heard a play—
	You break into some merry passion
	And so offend him, for I tell you, sirs,
	If you should smile he grows impatient.

A Player. Fear not, my lord, we can contain ourselves

Were he the veriest antic in the world.

Lord. Go, sirrah, take them to the buttery

And give them friendly welcome every one.

Let them want nothing that my house affords.

{*Exit one with the Players*}

Sirrah, go you to Barthol'mew my page

And see him dressed in all suits like a lady.

That done, conduct him to the drunkard's chamber

And call him "madam"; do him obeisance.

Tell him from me—as he will win my love—

He bear himself with honorable action

Such as he hath observed in noble ladies

Unto their lords, by them accomplishèd.

Such duty to the drunkard let him do

With soft low tongue and lowly courtesy,

And say, "What is't your honor will command
Wherein your lady and your humble wife
May show her duty and make known her love?"
And then, with kind embracements, tempting kisses,
And with declining head into his bosom,
Bid him shred tears, as being overjoyed
To see her noble lord restored to health
Who for this seven years hath esteemèd him
No better than a poor and loathsome beggar.
And if the boy have not a woman's gift
To rain a shower of commanded tears,
An onion will do well for such a shift,
Which in a napkin being close conveyed
Shall in despite enforce a watery eye.
See this dispatched with all the haste thou canst;
Anon I'll give thee more instructions.

   [Exit a Servingman]

I know the boy will well usurp the grace,
Voice, gait, and action of a gentlewoman.
I long to hear him call the drunkard husband,
And how my men will stay themselves from laughter
When they do homage to this simple peasant.
I'll in to counsel them; haply my presence
May well abate the over-merry spleen
Which otherwise would grow into extremes.

    [Exeunt]

[Enter aloft the Drunkard (Sly) with Attendants, some with apparel, basin and ewer, and some other appurtenances, with a Lord]

Sly. For God's sake, a pot of small ale!

First Servingman. Will't please your lordship drink a cup of sack?

Second Servingman. Will't please your honor taste of these conserves?

Third Servingman. What raiment will your honor wear today?

Sly. I am Christophero Sly; call not me "honor" nor "lordship." I ne'er drank sack in my life, and if you give me any conserves, give me conserves of beef. Ne'er ask me what raiment I'll wear, for I have no more doublets than backs, no more stockings than legs nor no more shoes than feet—nay, sometime more feet than shoes or such shoes as my toes look through the overleather.

Lord. Heaven cease this idle humor in your honor!
O that a mighty man of such descent,
Of such possessions and so high esteem,
Should be infusèd with so foul a spirit!

Sly. What, would you make me mad? Am not I Christopher Sly, old Sly's son of Burton-heath, by birth a peddler, by education a cardmaker, by transmutation a bearherd, and now by present profession a tinker? Ask Marian Hacket, the fat ale-wife of Wincot, if she know me not. If she say I am not fourteen pence on the score for sheer ale, score me up for the lying'st knave in Christendom. What, I am not bestraught! Here's—

Third Servingman. O, this it is that makes your lady mourn.

Second Servingman. O, this is it that makes your servants droop.

Lord. Hence comes it that your kindred shuns your house
As beaten hence by your strange lunacy.
O noble lord, bethink thee of thy birth,
Call home thy ancient thoughts from banishment
And banish hence these abject lowly dreams.
Look how thy servants do attend on thee,
Each in his office ready at thy beck.
Wilt thou have music? Hark, Apollo plays, *Music.*
And twenty cagèd nightingales do sing.
Or wilt thou sleep? We'll have thee to a couch
Softer and sweeter than the lustful bed

On purpose trimmed up for Semiramis.
Say thou wilt walk, we will bestrow the ground.
Or wilt thou ride? Thy horses shall be trapped,
Their harness studded all with gold and pearl.
Dost thou love hawking? Thou hast hawks will soar
Above the morning lark. Or wilt thou hunt?
Thy hounds shall make the welkin answer them
And fetch shrill echoes from the hollow earth.

First Servingman. Say thou wilt course, thy greyhounds are as swift
As breathed stags, ay, fleeter than the roe.

Second Servingman. Dost thou love pictures? We will fetch thee straight
Adonis painted by a running brook
And Cytherea all in sedges hid,
Which seem to move and wanton with her breath
Even as the waving sedges play with wind.

Lord. We'll show thee Io as she was a maid
And how she was beguilèd and surprised,
As lively painted as the deed was done.

Third Servingman.	Or Daphne roaming through a thorny wood,
	Scratching her legs that one shall swear she bleeds,
	And at that sight shall sad Apollo weep,
	So workmanly the blood and tears are drawn.
Lord.	Thou art a lord and nothing but a lord.
	Thou hast a lady far more beautiful
	Than any woman in this waning age.
First Servingman.	And till the tears that she hath shed for thee
	Like envious floods o'errun her lovely face,
	She was the fairest creature in the world,
	And yet she is inferior to none.
Sly.	Am I a lord, and have I such a lady?
	Or do I dream? Or have I dreamed till now?
	I do not sleep: I see, I hear, I speak,
	I smell sweet savors and I feel soft things.
	Upon my life, I am a lord indeed
	And not a tinker nor Christopher Sly.
	Well, bring our lady hither to our sight,
	And once again a pot o' th' smallest ale.

Second Servingman.	Will't please your mightiness to wash your hands?
	O, how we joy to see your wit restored!
	O, that once more you knew but what you are!
	These fifteen years you have been in a dream,
	Or when you waked so waked as if you slept.
Sly.	These fifteen years! By my fay, a goodly nap.
	But did I never speak of all that time?
First Servingman.	O yes, my lord, but very idle words,
	For though you lay here in this goodly chamber,
	Yet would you say ye were beaten out of door
	And rail upon the hostess of the house
	And say you would present her at the leet
	Because she brought stone jugs and no sealed quarts.
	Sometimes you would call out for Cicely Hacket.
Sly.	Ay, the woman's maid of the house.

Third Servingman.	Why, sir, you know no house nor no such maid
	Nor no such men as you have reckoned up,
	As Stephen Sly and old John Naps of Greece,
	And Peter Turph and Henry Pimpernell,
	And twenty more such names and men as these
	Which never were nor no man ever saw.
Sly.	Now, Lord be thankèd for my good amends!
All.	Amen.

[Enter the Page, as a Lady, with Attendants]

Sly.	I thank thee; thou shalt not lose by it.
Page.	How fares my noble lord?
Sly.	Marry, I fare well, for here is cheer enough.
	Where is my wife?
Page.	Here, noble lord. What is thy will with her?
Sly.	Are you my wife and will not call me husband?
	My men should call me "lord"; I am your goodman.
Page.	My husband and my lord, my lord and husband,
	I am your wife in all obedience.

Sly.	I know it well. What must I call her?
Lord.	Madam.
Sly.	Al'ce madam or Joan madam?
Lord.	Madam and nothing else. So lords call ladies.
Sly.	Madam wife, they say that I have dreamed
	And slept above some fifteen year or more.
Page.	Ay, and the time seems thirty unto me,
	Being all this time abandoned from your bed.
Sly.	'Tis much. Servants, leave me and her alone.
	Madam, undress you and come now to bed.
Page.	Thrice noble lord, let me entreat of you
	To pardon me yet for a night or two
	Or, if not so, until the sun be set.
	For your physicians have expressly charged,
	In peril to incur your former malady,
	That I should yet absent me from your bed.
	I hope this reason stands for my excuse.

Sly.   Ay, it stands so that I may hardly tarry so long, but I would be loath to fall into my dreams again. I will therefore tarry in despite of the flesh and the blood.

     [Enter a Messenger]

Messenger.   Your Honor's players, hearing your amendment,
Are come to play a pleasant comedy.
For so your doctors hold it very meet,
Seeing too much sadness hath congealed your blood,
And melancholy is the nurse of frenzy.
Therefore they thought it good you hear a play
And frame your mind to mirth and merriment,
Which bars a thousand harms and lengthens life.

Sly.   Marry, I will let them play it. Is not a comontie
a Christmas gambold or a tumbling trick?

Page.   No, my good lord, it is more pleasing stuff.

Sly.   What, household stuff?

Page.   It is a kind of history.

Sly.   Well, we'll see't. Come, madam wife, sit by my side
And let the world slip. We shell ne'er be younger.

ACT ONE

BAPTISTA

[Flourish. Enter Lucentio and his man Tranio]

Lucentio.   Tranio, since for the great desire I had

To see fair Padua, nursery of arts,

I am arrived for fruitful Lombardy,

The pleasant garden of great Italy,

And by my father's love and leave am armed

With his good will and thy good company,

My trusty servant well approved in all,

Here let us breathe and haply institute

A course of learning and ingenious studies.

Pisa, renownèd for grave citizens,

Gave me my being and my father first,

A merchant of great traffic through the world,

Vincentio, come of the Bentivolii.

Vincentio's son, brought up in Florence,

It shall become to serve all hopes conceived,

To deck his fortune with his virtuous deeds;
And therefore, Tranio, for the time I study,
Virtue and that part of philosophy
Will I apply that treats of happiness
By virtue specially to be achieved.
Tell me thy mind, for I have Pisa left
And am to Padua come, as he that leaves
A shallow plash to plunge him in the deep
And with satiety seeks to quench his thirst.

Tranio. *Mi perdonato,* gentle master mine,
I am in all affected as yourself,
Glad that you thus continue your resolve
To suck the sweets of sweet philosophy.
Only, good master, while we do admire
This virtue and this moral discipline,
Let's be no stoics nor no stocks, I pray,
Or so devote to Aristotle's checks
As Ovid be an outcast quite abjured.

Balk logic with acquaintance that you have

And practice rhetoric in your common talk.

Music and poesy use to quicken you.

The mathematics and the metaphysics,

Fall to them as you find your stomach serves you.

No profit grows where is no pleasure ta'en.

In brief, sir, study what you most affect.

Lucentio. Gramercies, Tranio, well dost thou advise.

If, Biondello, thou wert come ashore,

We could at once put us in readiness

And take a lodging fit to entertain

Such friends as time in Padua shall beget.

But stay awhile, what company is this?

Tranio. Master, some show to welcome us to town.

*[Enter Baptista with his two daughters, Kate and
Bianca; Gremio and a pantaloon; and Hortensio,
suitor to Bianca. Lucentio and Tranio stand by]*

Baptista.	Gentlemen, importune me no farther,
	For how I firmly am resolved you know,
	That is, not to bestow my youngest daughter
	Before I have a husband for the elder.
	If either of you both love Katherina,
	Because I know you well and love you well,
	Leave shall you have to court her at your pleasure.
Gremio.	To cart her rather. She's too rough for me.
	There, there, Hortensio, will you any wife?
Kate.	I pray you, sir, is it your will
	To make a stale of me amongst these mates?
Hortensio.	Mates, maid? How mean you that? No mates for you
	Unless you were of gentler, milder mold.
Kate.	I' faith, sir, you shall never need to fear:
	Iwis it is not halfway to her heart.
	But if it were, doubt not her care should be
	To comb your noddle with a three-legged stool
	And paint your face and use you like a fool.

Hortensio.	From all such devils, good Lord deliver us!
Gremio.	And me too, good Lord!
Tranio.	[*Aside*] Husht, master, here's some good pastime toward.
	That wench is stark mad or wonderful froward.
Lucentio.	[*Aside*] But in the other's silence do I see
	Maid's mild behavior and sobriety.
	Peace, Tranio.
Tranio.	[*Aside*] Well said, master. Mum, and gaze your fill.
Baptista.	Gentlemen, that I may soon make good
	What I have said: Bianca, get you in,
	And let it not displease thee, good Bianca,
	For I will love thee ne'er the less, my girl.
Kate.	A pretty peat! It is best
	Put finger in the eye, and she knew why.
Bianca.	Sister, content you in my discontent.
	Sir, to your pleasure humbly I subscribe.
	My books and instruments shall be my company,
	On them to look and practice by myself.
Lucentio.	[*Aside*] Hark, Tranio, thou mayst hear Minerva speak.

Hortensio. Signior Baptista, will you be so strange?
Sorry am I that our good will effects
Bianca's grief.

Gremio.   Why will you mew her up,
Signior Baptista, for this fiend of hell
And make her bear the penance of her tongue?

Baptista. Gentlemen, content ye. I am resolved.
Go in, Bianca.

    [Exit Bianca]

And for I know she taketh most delight
In music, instruments, and poetry,
Schoolmasters will I keep within my house,
Fit to instruct her youth. If you, Hortensio,
Or Signior Gremio, you, know any such,
Prefer them hither; for to cunning men
I will be very kind, and liberal
To mine own children in good bringing up.
And so, farewell. Katherina, you may stay,
For I have more to commune with Bianca.

    [Exit]

Kate. Why, and I trust I may go too, may I not?
What, shall I be appointed hours, as though, belike,
I knew not what to take and what to leave? Ha!
  [*Exit*]

Gremio. You may go to the devil's dam; your gifts are so good,
here's none will hold you. Their love is not so great,
Hortensio, but we may blow our nails together and fast
it fairly out. Our cake's dough on both sides. Farewell.
Yet for the love I bear my sweet Bianca, if I can by any
means light on a fit man to teach her that wherein she
delights, I will wish him to her father.

Hortensio. So will I, Signior Gremio. But a word, I pray. Though
the nature of our quarrel yet never brooked parle, know
now, upon advice, it toucheth us both—that we may yet
again have access to our fair mistress and be happy rivals
in Bianca's love—to labor and effect one thing specially.

Gremio. What's that, I pray?

Hortensio. Marry, sir, to get a husband for her sister.

Gremio. A husband! A devil.

Hortensio. I say, a husband.

Gremio. I say, a devil. Think'st thou, Hortensio, though her father be very rich, any man is so very a fool to be married to hell?

Hortensio. Tush, Gremio, though it pass your patience and mine to endure her loud alarums, why, man, there be good fellows in the world, and a man could light on them, would take her with all faults, and money enough.

Gremio. I cannot tell, but I had as lief take her dowry with this condition, to be whipped at the high cross every morning.

Hortensio. Faith, as you say, there's small choice in rotten apples. But come, since this bar in law makes us friends, it shall be so far forth friendly maintained, till by helping Baptista's eldest daughter to a husband, we set his youngest free for a husband, and then have to't afresh. Sweet Bianca! Happy man be his dole! He that runs fastest gets the ring. How say you, Signior Gremio?

Gremio. I am agreed, and would I had given him the best horse in Padua to begin his wooing, that would thoroughly woo her, wed her, and bed her and rid the house of her. Come on.

[Exeunt ambo. Manet, Tranio and Lucentio]

Tranio. I pray, sir, tell me, is it possible
That love should of a sudden take such hold?

Lucentio. O Tranio, till I found it to be true
I never thought it possible or likely.
But see, while idly I stood looking on,
I found the effect of love-in-idleness
And now in plainness do confess to thee,
That art to me as secret and as dear
As Anna to the Queen of Carthage was,
Tranio, I burn, I pine, I perish, Tranio,
If I achieve not this young modest girl.
Counsel me, Tranio, for I know thou canst.
Assist me, Tranio, for I know thou wilt.

Tranio.   Master, it is no time to chide you now.

Affection is not rated from the heart.

If love have touched you, naught remains but so,

"Redime te captum, quam queas minimo."

Lucentio.   Gramercies, lad, go forward. This contents.

The rest will comfort, for thy counsel's sound.

Tranio.   Master, you looked so longly on the maid,

Perhaps you marked not what's the pith of all.

Lucentio.   O yes, I saw sweet beauty in her face,

Such as the daughter of Agenor had,

That made great Jove to humble him to her hand

When with his knees he kissed the Cretan strond.

Tranio.   Saw you no more? Marked you not how her sister

Began to scold and raise up such a storm

That mortal ears might hardly endure the din?

Lucentio.   Tranio, I saw her coral lips to move

And with her breath she did perfume the air.

Sacred and sweet was all I saw in her.

Tranio.	Nay, then, 'tis time to stir him from his trance.
	I pray, awake, sir. If you love the maid,
	Bend thoughts and wits to achieve her. Thus it stands:
	Her elder sister is so curst and shrewd
	That till the father rid his hands of her,
	Master, your love must live a maid at home;
	And therefore has he closely mewed her up,
	Because she will not be annoyed with suitors.
Lucentio.	Ah, Tranio, what a cruel father's he!
	But art thou not advised he took some care
	To get her cunning schoolmasters to instruct her?
Tranio.	Ay, marry, am I, sir—and now 'tis plotted!
Lucentio.	I have it, Tranio!
Tranio.	Master, for my hand,
	Both our inventions meet and jump in one.
Lucentio.	Tell me thine first.
Tranio.	You will be schoolmaster
	And undertake the teaching of the maid.
	That's your device.
Lucentio.	It is. May it be done?

Tranio. Not possible, for who shall bear your part
And be in Padua here Vincentio's son?
Keep house and ply his book, welcome his friends,
Visit his countrymen and banquet them?

Lucentio. *Basta,* content thee, for I have it full.
We have not yet been seen in any house,
Nor can we be distinguished by our faces
For man or master. Then it follows thus:
Thou shalt be master, Tranio, in my stead,
Keep house and port and servants as I should.
I will some other be—some Florentine,
Some Neapolitan, or meaner man of Pisa.
'Tis hatched and shall be so. Tranio, at once
Uncase thee, take my colored hat and cloak.
When Biondello comes he waits on thee,
But I will charm him first to keep his tongue.

Tranio. So had you need.

In brief, sir, sith it your pleasure is

And I am tied to be obedient—

For so your father charged me at our parting;

"Be serviceable to my son," quoth he,

Although I think 'twas in another sense—

I am content to be Lucentio

Because so well I love Lucentio.

Lucentio. Tranio, be so, because Lucentio loves,

And let me be a slave, t'achieve that maid

Whose sudden sight hath thralled my wounded eye.

[Enter Biondello]

Here comes the rogue. Sirrah, where have you been?

Biondello. Where have I been? Nay, how now, where are you?

Master, has my fellow Tranio stol'n your clothes,

Or you stol'n his, or both? Pray, what's the news?

Lucentio. Sirrah, come hither. 'Tis no time to jest,
And therefore frame your manners to the time.
Your fellow Tranio, here, to save my life,
Puts my apparel and my count'nance on,
And I for my escape have put on his,
For in a quarrel since I came ashore
I killed a man and fear I was descried.
Wait you on him, I charge you, as becomes,
While I make way from hence to save my life.
You understand me?

Biondello. I, sir? Ne'er a whit.

Lucentio. And not a jot of Tranio in your mouth.
Tranio is changed into Lucentio.

Biondello. The better for him. Would I were so too.

Tranio. So could I, faith, boy, to have the next wish after,
That Lucentio indeed had Baptista's youngest daughter.
But, sirrah, not for my sake but your master's, I advise
You use your manners discreetly in all kind of companies.
When I am alone, why, then I am Tranio,
But in all places else your master, Lucentio.

Lucentio.	Tranio, let's go.
	One thing more rests, that thyself execute—
	To make one among these wooers. If thou ask me why,
	Sufficeth my reasons are both good and weighty.
	[Exeunt]
	[The Presenters above speaks]
First Servingman.	My lord, you nod; you do not mind the play.
Sly.	Yes, by Saint Anne, do I. A good matter, surely.
	Comes there any more of it?
Page.	My lord, 'tis but begun.
Sly.	'Tis a very excellent piece of work, madam lady.
	Would 'twere done!
	[They sit and mark]

[*Enter Petruchio and his man Grumio*]

Petruchio. Verona, for a while I take my leave
To see my friends in Padua, but of all
My best belovèd and approvèd friend,
Hortensio, and I trow this is his house.
Here, sirrah Grumio, knock, I say.

Grumio. Knock, sir? Whom should I knock?
Is there any man has rebused your worship?

Petruchio. Villain, I say, knock me here soundly.

Grumio. Knock you here, sir? Why, sir, what am I, sir, that I
should knock you here, sir?

Petruchio. Villain, I say, knock me at this gate
And rap me well or I'll knock your knave's pate.

Grumio. My master is grown quarrelsome. I should knock you first,
And then I know after who comes by the worst.

GREMIO

Petruchio.	Will it not be?
	Faith, sirrah, and you'll not knock, I'll ring it;
	I'll try how you can *sol, fa,* and sing it.
	[*He wrings him by the ears*]
Grumio.	Help, masters, help! My master is mad.
Petruchio.	Now, knock when I bid you, sirrah villain.
	[*Enter Hortensio*]
Hortensio.	How now, what's the matter? My old friend Grumio, and my good friend Petruchio! How do you all at Verona?
Petruchio.	Signior Hortensio, come you to part the fray?
	Con tutto il cuore ben trovato,
Hortensio.	*Alla nostra casa ben venuto, molto honorato signior mio Petruchio.*
	Rise, Grumio, rise. We will compound this quarrel.

Grumio. Nay, 'tis no matter, sir, what he 'leges in Latin. If this be not a lawful cause for me to leave his service—look you, sir, he bid me knock him and rap him soundly, sir. Well, was it fit for a servant to use his master so, being perhaps, for aught I see, two-and-thirty, a peep out? Whom would to God I had well knocked at first, Then had not Grumio come by the worst.

Petruchio. A senseless villain! Good Hortensio,
I bade the rascal knock upon your gate
And could not get him for my heart to do it.

Grumio. Knock at the gate? O heavens! Spake you not these words plain, "Sirrah, knock me here, rap me here, knock me well, and knock me soundly"? And come you now with "knocking at the gate"?

Petruchio. Sirrah, be gone or talk not, I advise you.

Hortensio. Petruchio, patience, I am Grumio's pledge.
Why, this's a heavy chance 'twixt him and you,
Your ancient, trusty, pleasant servant Grumio.
And tell me now, sweet friend, what happy gale
Blows you to Padua here from Old Verona?

Petruchio. Such wind as scatters young men through the world
To seek their fortunes farther than at home,
Where small experience grows. But in a few,
Signior Hortensio, thus it stands with me:
Antonio my father is deceased,
And I have thrust myself into this maze,
Happily to wive and thrive as best I may.
Crowns in my purse I have and goods at home
And so am come abroad to see the world.

Hortensio. Petruchio, shall I then come roundly to thee
And wish thee to a shrewd ill-favored wife?
Thou'ldst thank me but a little for my counsel—
And yet I'll promise thee she shall be rich,
And very rich—but thou'rt too much my friend,
And I'll not wish thee to her.

Petruchio. Signior Hortensio, 'twixt such friends as we
Few words suffice; and therefore if thou know
One rich enough to be Petruchio's wife—
As wealth is burthen of my wooing dance—
Be she as foul as was Florentius' love,
As old as Sibyl, and as curst and shrewd
As Socrates' Xanthippe or a worse,
She moves me not, or not removes, at least,
Affection's edge in me, were she as rough
As are the swelling Adriatic seas.
I come to wive it wealthily in Padua;
If wealthily, then happily in Padua.

Grumio. Nay, look you, sir, he tells you flatly what his mind is.
Why, give him gold enough and marry him to a puppet
or an aglet-baby or an old trot with ne'er a tooth in her
head, though she have as many diseases as two-and-fifty
horses. Why, nothing comes amiss so money comes
withal.

Hortensio. Petruchio, since we are stepped thus far in,
I will continue that I broached in jest.
I can, Petruchio, help thee to a wife
With wealth enough and young and beauteous,
Brought up as best becomes a gentlewoman.
Her only fault—and that is faults enough—
Is that she is intolerable curst
And shrewd and froward, so beyond all measure
That were my state far worser than it is,
I would not wed her for a mine of gold.

Petruchio. Hortensio, peace. Thou know'st not gold's effect.
Tell me her father's name, and 'tis enough,
For I will board her though she chide as loud
As thunder when the clouds in autumn crack.

Hortensio. Her father is Baptista Minola,
An affable and courteous gentleman.
Her name is Katherina Minola,
Renowned in Padua for her scolding tongue.

Petruchio. I know her father though I know not her,
And he knew my deceasèd father well.
I will not sleep, Hortensio, till I see her,
And therefore let me be thus bold with you,
To give you over at this first encounter
Unless you will accompany me thither.

Grumio. I pray you, sir, let him go while the humor lasts. A my word, and she knew him as well as I do, she would think scolding would do little good upon him. She may perhaps call him half a score knaves or so—why, that's nothing. And he begin once, he'll rail in his rope-tricks. I'll tell you what, sir, and she stand him but a little, he will throw a figure in her face and so disfigure her with it that she shall have no more eyes to see withal than a cat. You know him not, sir.

Hortensio.	Tarry, Petruchio, I must go with thee,
	For in Baptista's keep my treasure is.
	He hath the jewel of my life in hold,
	His youngest daughter, beautiful Bianca,
	And her withholds from me and other more,
	Suitors to her and rivals in my love,
	Supposing it a thing impossible,
	For those defects I have before rehearsed,
	That ever Katherina will be wooed.
	Therefore this order hath Baptista ta'en,
	That none shall have access unto Bianca
	Till Katherine the curst have got a husband.
Grumio.	Katherine the curst!
	A title for a maid of all titles the worst.
Hortensio.	Now shall my friend Petruchio do me grace
	And offer me, disguised in sober robes,
	To old Baptista as a schoolmaster
	Well seen in music, to instruct Bianca,
	That so I may, by this device, at least
	Have leave and leisure to make love to her
	And unsuspected court her by herself.

[Enter Gremio, and Lucentio dis-
guised as a schoolmaster, Cambio]

Grumio. Here's no knavery! See, to beguile the old folks, how the
young folks lay their heads together! Master, master,
look about you. Who goes there, ha?

Hortensio. Peace, Grumio. It is the rival of my love.
Petruchio, stand by awhile.

[They eavesdrop]

Grumio. A proper stripling, and an amorous!

Gremio. O, very well, I have perused the note.
Hark you, sir, I'll have them very fairly bound—
All books of love, see that at any hand,
And see you read no other lectures to her.
You understand me. Over and beside
Signior Baptista's liberality,
I'll mend it with a largess. Take your paper too
And let me have them very well perfumed,
For she is sweeter than perfume itself
To whom they go to. What will you read to her?

Lucentio.	Whate'er I read to her, I'll plead for you
	As for my patron, stand you so assured,
	As firmly as yourself were still in place—
	Yea, and perhaps with more successful words
	Than you unless you were a scholar, sir.
Gremio.	O this learning, what a thing it is!
Grumio.	[*Aside*] O this woodcock, what an ass it is!
Petruchio.	Peace, sirrah!
Hortensio.	Grumio, mum! [*Coming forward*] God save you, Signior Gremio.
Gremio.	And you are well met, Signior Hortensio.
	Trow you whither I am going? To Baptista Minola.
	I promised to inquire carefully
	About a schoolmaster for the fair Bianca,
	And, by good fortune, I have lighted well
	On this young man—for learning and behavior
	Fit for her turn, well read in poetry
	And other books, good ones I warrant ye.

Hortensio.	'Tis well. And I have met a gentleman
	Hath promised me to help me to another,
	A fine musician to instruct our mistress.
	So shall I no whit be behind in duty
	To fair Bianca, so beloved of me.
Gremio.	Beloved of me, and that my deeds shall prove.
Grumio.	[Aside] And that his bags shall prove.
Hortensio.	Gremio, 'tis now no time to vent our love.
	Listen to me, and if you speak me fair,
	I'll tell you news indifferent good for either.
	Here is a gentleman whom by chance I met,
	Upon agreement from us to his liking,
	Will undertake to woo curst Katherine,
	Yea, and to marry her if her dowry please.
Gremio.	So said, so done, is well.
	Hortensio, have you told him all her faults?
Petruchio.	I know she is an irksome, brawling scold;
	If that be all, masters, I hear no harm.

Gremio.	No, say'st me so, friend? What countryman?
Petruchio.	Born in Verona, old Antonio's son.
	My father dead, my fortune lives for me,
	And I do hope good days and long to see.
Gremio.	O, sir, such a life with such a wife were strange.
	But if you have a stomach, to't a God's name;
	You shall have me assisting you in all.
	But will you woo this wildcat?
Petruchio.	Will I live?
Grumio.	[Aside] Will he woo her? Ay, or I'll hang her.
Petruchio.	Why came I hither but to that intent?
	Think you a little din can daunt mine ears?
	Have I not in my time heard lions roar?
	Have I not heard the sea, puffed up with winds,
	Rage like an angry boar chafèd with sweat?
	Have I not heard great ordnance in the field
	And heaven's artillery thunder in the skies?

Have I not in a pitchèd battle heard

Loud 'larums, neighing steeds, and trumpets' clang?

And do you tell me of a woman's tongue,

That gives not half so great a blow to hear

As will a chestnut in a farmer's fire?

Tush, tush, fear boys wtih bugs.

Grumio. [Aside]   For he fears none.

Gremio. Hortensio, hark.

This gentleman is happily arrived,

My mind presumes, for his own good and ours.

Hortensio. I promised we would be contributors

And bear his charge of wooing, whatsoe'er.

Gremio. And so we will, provided that he win her.

Grumio. [Aside] I would I were as sure of a good dinner.

[Enter Tranio brave, as Lucentio, and Biondello]

Tranio. Gentlemen, God save you. If I may be bold,

Tell me, I beseech you, which is the readiest way

To the house of Signior Baptista Minola?

Biondello.	He that has the two fair daughters? Is't he you mean?
Tranio.	Even he, Biondello.
Gremio.	Hark you, sir. You mean not her to—
Tranio.	Perhaps, him and her, sir. What have you to do?
Petruchio.	Not her that chides, sir, at any hand, I pray.
Tranio.	I love no chiders, sir. Biondello, let's away.
Lucentio.	[*Aside*] Well begun, Tranio.
Hortensio.	Sir, a word ere you go.
	Are you a suitor to the maid you talk of, yea or no?
Tranio.	And if I be, sir, is it any offense?
Gremio.	No, if without more words you will get you hence.
Tranio.	Why, sir, I pray, are not the streets as free
	For me as for you?
Gremio.	But so is not she.

Tranio.	For what reason, I beseech you?
Gremio.	For this reason, if you'll know,
	That she's the choice love of Signior Gremio.
Hortensio.	That she's the chosen of Signior Hortensio.
Tranio.	Softly, my masters! If you be gentlemen,
	Do me this right: hear me with patience.
	Baptista is a noble gentleman
	To whom my father is not all unknown,
	And were his daughter fairer than she is,
	She may more suitors have, and me for one.
	Fair Leda's daughter had a thousand wooers;
	Then well one more may fair Bianca have.
	And so she shall. Lucentio shall make one,
	Though Paris came in hope to speed alone.

Gremio.	What, this gentleman will out-talk us all.
Lucentio.	Sir, give him head. I know he'll prove a jade.
Petruchio.	Hortensio, to what end are all these words?
Hortensio.	Sir, let me be so bold as ask you,
	Did you yet ever see Baptista's daughter?
Tranio.	No, sir, but hear I do that he hath two,
	The one as famous for a scolding tongue
	As is the other for beauteous modesty.
Petruchio.	Sir, sir, the first's for me; let her go by.
Gremio.	Yea, leave that labor to great Hercules,
	And let it be more than Alcides' twelve.
Petruchio.	Sir, understand you this of me in sooth:
	The youngest daughter, whom you hearken for,
	Her father keeps from all access of suitors
	And will not promise her to any man
	Until the elder sister first be wed.
	The younger then is free, and not before.

Tranio.	If it be so, sir, that you are the man
	Must stead us all, and me amongst the rest,
	And if you break the ice and do this feat,
	Achieve the elder, set the younger free
	For our access, whose hap shall be to have her
	Will not so graceless be to be ingrate.
Hortensio.	Sir, you say well, and well you do conceive,
	And since you do profess to be a suitor,
	You must, as we do, gratify this gentleman
	To whom we all rest generally beholding.
Tranio.	Sir, I shall not be slack, in sign whereof,
	Please ye we may contrive this afternoon
	And quaff carouses to our mistress' health
	And do as adversaries do in law,
	Strive mightily but eat and drink as friends.

Grumio, Biondello. O excellent motion! Fellows, let's be gone.

Hortensio. The motion's good indeed, and be it so.

Petruchio, I shall be your *ben venuto*.

[*Exeunt*]

ACT TWO

BIANCA

SCENE I
IN BAPTISTA'S HOUSE

[Enter Kate and Bianca with her hands tied]

Bianca.   Good sister, wrong me not nor wrong yourself
            To make a bondmaid and a slave of me.
            That I disdain. But for these other gawds,
            Unbind my hands, I'll pull them off myself,
            Yea, all my raiment, to my petticoat,
            Or what you will command me will I do,
            So well I know my duty to my elders.

Kate.   Of all thy suitors, here I charge thee, tell
            Whom thou lov'st best. See thou dissemble not.

Bianca.   Believe me, sister, of all the men alive
            I never yet beheld that special face
            Which I could fancy more than any other.

Kate.   Minion, thou liest. Is't not Hortensio?

Bianca.   If you affect him, sister, here I swear
            I'll plead for you myself but you shall have him.

Kate.	O then, belike, you fancy riches more:
	You will have Gremio to keep you fair.
Bianca.	Is it for him you do envy me so?
	Nay, then you jest, and now I well perceive
	You have but jested with me all this while.
	I prithee, sister Kate, untie my hands.
Kate.	If that be jest then all the rest was so.
	[Strikes her]
	[Enter Baptista]
Baptista.	Why, how now, dame, whence grows this insolence?
	Bianca, stand aside. Poor girl, she weeps.
	Go ply thy needle; meddle not with her.
	For shame, thou hilding of a devilish spirit,
	Why dost thou wrong her that did ne'er wrong thee?
	When did she cross thee with a bitter word?
Kate.	Her silence flouts me and I'll be revenged.
	[Flies after Bianca]
Baptista.	What, in my sight? Bianca, get thee in.
	[Exit Bianca]

Kate. What, will you not suffer me? Nay, now I see
She is your treasure, she must have a husband;
I must dance barefoot on her wedding day,
And, for your love to her, lead apes in hell.
Talk not to me; I will go sit and weep
Till I can find occasion of revenge.
    [Exit]

Baptista. Was ever gentleman thus grieved as I?
But who comes here?

    *[Enter Gremio, Lucentio in the habit of a mean
    man Cambio, Petruchio, with Hortensio as a
    music teacher, Litio, and Tranio as Lucentio,
    with his boy Biondello bearing a lute and books]*

Gremio. Good morrow, neighbor Baptista.

Baptista. Good morrow, neighbor Gremio. God save you, gentlemen.

Petruchio. And you, good sir. Pray, have you not a daughter
Called Katherina, fair and virtuous?

Baptista. I have a daughter, sir, called Katherina.

Gremio. *[Aside]* You are too blunt; go to it orderly.

Petruchio.   [*Aside*] You wrong me, Signior Gremio, give me leave.

           [*To Baptista*] I am a gentleman of Verona, sir,

           That, hearing of her beauty and her wit,

           Her affability and bashful modesty,

           Her wondrous qualities and mild behavior,

           Am bold to show myself a forward guest

           Within your house, to make mine eye the witness

           Of that report which I so oft have heard.

           And, for an entrance to my entertainment,

           I do present you with a man of mine,

              [*Presenting Hortensio*]

           Cunning in music and the mathematics,

           To instruct her fully in those sciences,

           Whereof I know she is not ignorant.

           Accept of him, or else you do me wrong.

           His name is Litio, born in Mantua.

Baptista.   Y'are welcome, sir, and he for your good sake.

           But for my daughter Katherine, this I know,

           She is not for your turn, the more my grief.

Petruchio. I see you do not mean to part with her,
Or else you like not of my company.

Baptista. Mistake me not; I speak but as I find.
Whence are you, sir? What may I call your name?

Petruchio. Petruchio is my name, Antonio's son,
A man well known throughout all Italy.

Baptista. I know him well. You are welcome for his sake.

Gremio. Saving your tale, Petruchio, I pray,
Let us, that are poor petitioners, speak too.
Backare, you are marvelous forward.

Petruchio. O pardon me, Signior Gremio, I would fain be doing.

Gremio. I doubt it not, sir, but you will curse your wooing.
Neighbor, this is a gift very grateful, I am sure of it. To express the like kindness myself, that have been more kindly beholding to you than any, freely give unto you this young scholar [*Presenting Lucentio*] that hath been long studying at Rheims—as cunning in Greek, Latin, and other languages, as the other in music and mathematics. His name is Cambio. Pray accept his service.

Baptista. A thousand thanks, Signior Gremio. Welcome, good
Cambio. [*To Tranio*] But, gentle sir, methinks you walk
like a stranger. May I be so bold to know the cause of
your coming?

Tranio. Pardon me, sir, the boldness is mine own,
That, being a stranger in this city here,
Do make myself a suitor to your daughter,
Unto Bianca, fair and virtuous.
Nor is your firm resolve unknown to me
In the preferment of the eldest sister.
This liberty is all that I request,
That, upon knowledge of my parentage,
I may have welcome 'mongst the rest that woo
And free access and favor as the rest.
And, toward the education of your daughters
I here bestow a simple instrument,
And this small packet of Greek and Latin books.
If you accept them, then their worth is great.

Baptista.   [*Looking at books*] Lucentio is your name.

Of whence, I pray?

Tranio.   Of Pisa, sir, son to Vincentio.

Baptista.   A mighty man of Pisa; by report

I know him well. You are very welcome, sir.

[*To Hortensio*] Take you the lute,

[*To Lucentio*] and you the set of books;

You shall go see your pupils presently.

Holla, within!

[*Enter a Servant*]

Sirrah, lead these gentlemen

To my daughters and tell them both

These are their tutors; bid them use them well.

[*Exit Servant, with Lucentio, followed by Hortensio, and Biondello*]

We will go walk a little in the orchard

And then to dinner. You are passing welcome,

And so I pray you all to think yourselves.

Petruchio. Signior Baptista, my business asketh haste,
And every day I cannot come to woo.
You knew my father well, and in him me,
Left solely heir to all his lands and goods,
Which I have bettered rather than decreased.
Then tell me, if I get your daughter's love
What dowry shall I have with her to wife?

Baptista. After my death the one half of my lands,
And in possession twenty thousand crowns.

Petruchio. And, for that dowry, I'll assure her of
Her widowhood, be it that she survive me,
In all my lands and leases whatsoever.
Let specialties be therefore drawn between us
That covenants may be kept on either hand.

Baptista. Ay, when the special thing is well obtained,
That is, her love, for that is all in all.

Petruchio.	Why, that is nothing, for I tell you, father,
	I am as peremptory as she proud-minded.
	And where two raging fires meet together
	They do consume the thing that feeds their fury.
	Though little fire grows great with little wind,
	Yet extreme gusts will blow out fire and all.
	So I to her, and so she yields to me,
	For I am rough and woo not like a babe.
Baptista.	Well mayst thou woo, and happy be thy speed!
	But be thou armed for some unhappy words.
Petruchio.	Ay, to the proof, as mountains are for winds
	That shakes not, though they blow perpetually.
	[Enter Hortensio with his head broke]
Baptista.	How now, my friend, why dost thou look so pale?
Hortensio.	For fear, I promise you, if I look pale.
Baptista.	What, will my daughter prove a good musician?
Hortensio.	I think she'll sooner prove a soldier.
	Iron may hold her, but never lutes.
Baptista.	Why, then thou canst not break her to the lute?

Hortensio.	Why, no, for she hath broke the lute to me.
	I did but tell her she mistook her frets
	And bowed her hand to teach her fingering,
	When, with a most impatient devilish spirit,
	"Frets, call you these?" quoth she; "I'll fume with them."
	And with that word she stroke me on the head,
	And through the instrument my pate made way.
	And there I stood amazèd for a while
	As on a pillory, looking through the lute,
	While she did call me rascal, fiddler,
	And twangling Jack, with twenty such vile terms
	As had she studied to misuse me so.
Petruchio.	Now, by the world, it is a lusty wench!
	I love her ten times more than e'er I did.
	O how I long to have some chat with her!
Baptista.	[*To Hortensio*] Well, go with me, and be not so discomfited.
	Proceed in practice with my younger daughter;
	She's apt to learn and thankful for good turns.
	Signior Petruchio, will you go with us
	Or shall I send my daughter Kate to you?

[*Exit Baptista, with Gremio, Tranio,*
and Hortensio. Manet Petruchio]

Petruchio.   I pray you do. I'll attend her here

And woo her with some spirit when she comes.

Say that she rail, why then I'll tell her plain

She sings as sweetly as a nightingale.

Say that she frown, I'll say she looks as clear

As morning roses newly washed with dew.

Say she be mute and will not speak a word,

Then I'll commend her volubility

And say she uttereth piercing eloquence.

If she do bid me pack, I'll give her thanks

As though she bid me stay by her a week.

If she deny to wed, I'll crave the day

When I shall ask the banns and when be marrièd.

But here she comes, and now, Petruchio, speak.

    [*Enter Kate*]

Good morrow, Kate, for that's your name, I hear.

Kate.   Well have you heard, but something hard of hearing.

           They call me Katherine that do talk of me.

Petruchio.   You lie, in faith, for you are called plain Kate,

           And bonny Kate, and sometimes Kate the curst.

           But, Kate, the prettiest Kate in Christendom,

           Kate of Kate Hall, my super-dainty Kate,

           For dainties are all Kates, and therefore, Kate,

           Take this of me, Kate of my consolation.

           Hearing thy mildness praised in every town,

           Thy virtues spoke of, and thy beauty sounded—

           Yet not so deeply as to thee belongs—

           Myself am moved to woo thee for my wife.

Kate.   Moved! In good time, let him that moved you hither

           Remove you hence. I knew you at the first

           You were a movable.

Petruchio.   Why, what's a movable?

Kate.   A joint stool.

Petruchio.   Thou hast hit it; come sit on me.

Kate.	Asses are made to bear and so are you.
Petruchio.	Women are made to bear and so are you.
Kate.	No such jade as you, if me you mean.
Petruchio.	Alas, good Kate, I will not burden thee,
	For, knowing thee to be but young and light—
Kate.	Too light for such a swain as you to catch
	And yet as heavy as my weight should be.
Petruchio.	Should be! Should—buzz!
Kate.	Well ta'en, and like a buzzard.
Petruchio.	O slow-winged turtle, shall a buzzard take thee?
Kate.	Ay, for a turtle, as he takes a buzzard.
Petruchio.	Come, come; you wasp, i' faith you are too angry.
Kate.	If I be waspish, best beware my sting.
Petruchio.	My remedy is then to pluck it out.
Kate.	Ay, if the fool could find it where it lies.
Petruchio.	Who knows not where a wasp does wear his sting?
	In his tail.
Kate.	In his tongue.
Petruchio.	Whose tongue?

Kate.	Yours, if you talk of tales, and so farewell.
Petruchio.	What, with my tongue in your tail? Nay, come again.
	Good Kate, I am a gentleman—
Kate.	That I'll try.

[She strikes him]

Petruchio.	I swear I'll cuff you if you strike again.
Kate.	So you may lose your arms:
	If you strike me you are no gentleman,
	And if no gentleman, why then no arms.
Petruchio.	A herald, Kate? O, put me in thy books.
Kate.	What is your crest? A coxcomb?
Petruchio.	A combless cock, so Kate will be my hen.
Kate.	No cock of mine; you crow too like a craven.
Petruchio.	Nay, come, Kate, come, you must not look so sour.
Kate.	It is my fashion when I see a crab.
Petruchio.	Why, here's no crab, and therefore look not sour.
Kate.	There is, there is.
Petruchio.	Then show it me.
Kate.	Had I a glass I would.

Petruchio.	What, you mean my face?
Kate.	Well aimed of
	such a young one.
Petruchio.	Now, by Saint George, I am too young for you.
Kate.	Yet you are withered.
Petruchio.	'Tis with cares.
Kate.	I care not.
Petruchio.	Nay, hear you, Kate, in sooth you scape not so.
Kate.	I chafe you if I tarry. Let me go.
Petruchio.	No, not a whit. I find you passing gentle.

'Twas told me you were rough and coy and sullen,
And now I find report a very liar,
For thou art pleasant, gamesome, passing courteous,
But slow in speech, yet sweet as springtime flowers.
Thou canst not frown, thou canst not look askance,
Nor bite the lip as angry wenches will,
Nor hast thou pleasure to be cross in talk,

But thou with mildness entertain'st thy wooers,
With gentle conference, soft and affable.
Why does the world report that Kate doth limp?
O sland'rous world! Kate like the hazel-twig
Is straight and slender, and as brown in hue
As hazelnuts and sweeter than the kernels.
O, let me see thee walk. Thou dost not halt.

Kate. Go, fool, and whom thou keep'st command.

Petruchio. Did ever Dian so become a grove
As Kate this chamber with her princely gait?
O, be thou Dian and let her be Kate,
And then let Kate be chaste and Dian sportful!

Kate. Where did you study all this goodly speech?

Petruchio. It is extempore, from my mother-wit.

Kate. A witty mother! Witless else her son.

Petruchio. Am I not wise?

Kate. Yes, keep you warm.

Petruchio.   Marry, so I mean, sweet Katherine, in thy bed.
And therefore, setting all this chat aside,
Thus in plain terms: your father hath consented
That you shall be my wife, your dowry 'greed on,
And will you, nill you, I will marry you.
Now, Kate, I am a husband for your turn,
For, by this light, whereby I see thy beauty—
Thy beauty that doth make me like thee well—
Thou must be married to no man but me.
   [Enter Baptista, Gremio, Tranio]
For I am he am born to tame you, Kate,
And bring you from a wild Kate to a Kate
Conformable as other household Kates.
Here comes your father. Never make denial;
I must and will have Katherine to my wife.

Baptista.   Now, Signior Petruchio, how speed you with my daughter?

Petruchio.	How but well, sir? How but well?
	It were impossible I should speed amiss.
Baptista.	Why, how now, daughter Katherine, in your dumps?
Kate.	Call you me daughter? Now, I promise you
	You have showed a tender fatherly regard
	To wish me wed to one half lunatic,
	A madcap ruffian and a swearing Jack
	That thinks with oaths to face the matter out.
Petruchio.	Father, 'tis thus: yourself and all the world
	That talked of her have talked amiss of her.
	If she be curst it is for policy,
	For she's not froward but modest as the dove.
	She is not hot but temperate as the morn;
	For patience she will prove a second Grissel
	And Roman Lucrece for her chastity.
	And to conclude, we have 'greed so well together
	That upon Sunday is the wedding day.
Kate.	I'll see thee hanged on Sunday first.

Gremio.	Hark, Petruchio, she says she'll see thee hanged first.
Tranio.	Is this your speeding? Nay, then good night our part!
Petruchio.	Be patient, gentlemen, I choose her for myself.
	If she and I be pleased, what's that to you?
	'Tis bargained 'twixt us twain, being alone,
	That she shall still be curst in company.
	I tell you, 'tis incredible to believe
	How much she loves me. O, the kindest Kate,
	She hung about my neck, and kiss on kiss
	She vied so fast, protesting oath on oath,
	That in a twink she won me to her love.
	O, you are novices. 'Tis a world to see
	How tame, when men and women are alone,
	A meacock wretch can make the curstest shrew.
	Give me thy hand, Kate. I will unto Venice
	To buy apparel 'gainst the wedding day.
	Provide the feast, father, and bid the guests;
	I will be sure my Katherine shall be fine.
Baptista.	I know not what to say, but give me your hands.
	God send you joy, Petruchio! 'Tis a match.

Gremio, Tranio.	Amen, say we. We will be witnesses.
Petruchio.	Father, and wife, and gentlemen, adieu.
	I will to Venice; Sunday comes apace.
	We will have rings and things and fine array,
	And, kiss me, Kate, "We will be married a Sunday."
	[Exit Petruchio and Kate]
Gremio.	Was ever match clapped up so suddenly?
Baptista.	Faith, gentlemen, now I play a merchant's part
	And venture madly on a desperate mart.
Tranio.	'Twas a commodity lay fretting by you;
	'Twill bring you gain or perish on the seas.
Baptista.	The gain I seek is quiet in the match.
Gremio.	No doubt but he hath got a quiet catch.
	But now, Baptista, to your younger daughter;
	Now is the day we long have lookèd for.
	I am your neighbor and was suitor first.
Tranio.	And I am one that love Bianca more
	Than words can witness or your thoughts can guess.

GRUMIO

Gremio.	Youngling, thou canst not love so dear as I.
Tranio.	Graybeard, thy love doth freeze.
Gremio.	But thine doth fry.
	Skipper, stand back, 'tis age that nourisheth.
Tranio.	But youth in ladies' eyes that flourisheth.
Baptista.	Content you, gentlemen; I will compound this strife.
	'Tis deeds must win the prize, and he of both
	That can assure my daughter greatest dower
	Shall have my Bianca's love.
	Say, Signior Gremio, what can you assure her?
Gremio.	First, as you know, my house within the city
	Is richly furnishèd with plate and gold,
	Basins and ewers to lave her dainty hands;
	My hangings all of Tyrian tapestry;
	In ivory coffers I have stuffed my crowns,
	In cypress chests my arras counterpoints,
	Costly apparel, tents, and canopies,
	Fine linen, Turkey cushions bossed with pearl,
	Valance of Venice gold in needlework,
	Pewter and brass, and all things that belongs

To house or housekeeping. Then, at my farm
I have a hundred milch-kine to the pail,
Six score fat oxen standing in my stalls
And all things answerable to this portion.
Myself am struck in years, I must confess,
And if I die tomorrow, this is hers,
If whilst I live she will be only mine.

Tranio. That "only" came well in. Sir, list to me.
I am my father's heir and only son.
If I may have your daughter to my wife,
I'll leave her houses three or four as good,
Within rich Pisa walls, as any one
Old Signior Gremio has in Padua,
Besides two thousand ducats by the year
Of fruitful land, all which shall be her jointure.
What, have I pinched you, Signior Gremio?

Gremio.	[*Aside*] Two thousand ducats by the year of land!
	My land amounts not to so much in all.
	[*To others*] That she shall have besides an argosy
	That now is lying in Marcellus' road.
	What, have I choked you with an argosy?
Tranio.	Gremio, 'tis known my father hath no less
	Than three great argosies, besides two galliasses
	And twelve tight galleys. These I will assure her
	And twice as much, whate'er thou off'rest next.
Gremio.	Nay, I have off'red all. I have no more,
	And she can have no more than all I have.
	If you like me, she shall have me and mine.
Tranio.	Why, then the maid is mine from all the world
	By your firm promise. Gremio is outvied.
Baptista.	I must confess your offer is the best,
	And let your father make her the assurance,
	She is your own; else you must pardon me.
	If you should die before him, where's her dower?

Tranio.   That's but a cavil. He is old, I young.

Gremio.   And may not young men die as well as old?

Baptista.   Well, gentlemen,
I am thus resolved. On Sunday next, you know,
My daughter Katherine is to be married.
Now on the Sunday following shall Bianca
Be bride to you if you make this assurance;
If not, to Signior Gremio.
And so I take my leave and thank you both.
   [*Exit*]

Gremio.   Adieu, good neighbor. Now I fear thee not.
Sirrah young gamester, your father were a fool
To give thee all and in his waning age
Set foot under thy table. Tut, a toy!
An old Italian fox is not so kind, my boy.
   [*Exit*]

Tranio. A vengeance on your crafty withered hide!
Yet I have faced it with a card of ten.
'Tis in my head to do my master good.
I see no reason but supposed Lucentio
Must get a father, called "supposed Vincentio,"
And that's a wonder. Fathers commonly
Do get their children, but in this case of wooing
A child shall get a sire if I fail not of my cunning.
[Exit]

ACT THREE

LUCENTIO

SCENE I

PADUA. IN BAPTISTA'S HOUSE

[Enter Lucentio as Cambio, with
Hortensio as Litio, and Bianca]

Lucentio. Fiddler, forbear. You grow too forward, sir.
　　　　　Have you so soon forgot the entertainment
　　　　　Her sister Katherine welcomed you withal?

Hortensio. But, wrangling pedant, this is
　　　　　The patroness of heavenly harmony.
　　　　　Then give me leave to have prerogative,
　　　　　And when in music we have spent an hour,
　　　　　Your lecture shall have leisure for as much.

Lucentio. Preposterous ass, that never read so far
　　　　　To know the cause why music was ordained!
　　　　　Was it not to refresh the mind of man
　　　　　After his studies or his usual pain?
　　　　　Then give me leave to read philosophy,
　　　　　And while I pause, serve in your harmony.

Hortensio.	Sirrah, I will not bear these braves of thine.
Bianca.	Why, gentlemen, you do me double wrong
	To strive for that which resteth in my choice.
	I am no breeching scholar in the schools.
	I'll not be tied to hours nor 'pointed times,
	But learn my lessons as I please myself.
	And, to cut off all strife, here sit we down.
	[To Hortensio]
	Take you your instrument, play you the whiles;
	His lecture will be done ere you have tuned.
Hortensio.	You'll leave his lecture when I am in tune?
Lucentio.	That will be never. Tune your instrument.
Bianca.	Where left we last?
Lucentio.	Here, madam:
	Hic ibat Simois, hic est Sigeia tellus,
	Hic steterat Priami regia celsa senis.
Bianca.	Conster them.

Lucentio.	*Hic ibat,* as I told you before, *Simois,* I am Lucentio, *hic est,* son unto Vincentio of Pisa, *Sigeia tellus,* disguised thus to get your love, *Hic steterat,* and that Lucentio that comes a wooing, *Priami,* is my man Tranio, *regia,* bearing my port, *celsa senis,* that we might beguile the old pantaloon.
Hortensio.	[*Breaks in*] Madam, my instrument's in tune.
Bianca.	Let's hear. O fie, the treble jars.
Lucentio.	Spit in the hole, man, and tune again.
Bianca.	Now let me see if I can conster it. *Hic ibat Simois,* I know you not, *hic est Sigeia tellus,* I trust you not, *Hic steterat Priami,* take heed he hear us not, *regia,* presume not, *celsa senis,* despair not.
Hortensio.	[*Breaks in again*] Madam, 'tis now in tune.
Lucentio.	All but the bass.
Hortensio.	The bass is right; 'tis the base knave that jars. [*Aside*] How fiery and forward our pedant is! Now, for my life, the knave doth court my love. *Pedascule,* I'll watch you better yet.

Bianca.	In time I may believe, yet I mistrust.
Lucentio.	Mistrust it not, for sure Aeacides
	Was Ajax, called so from his grandfather.
Bianca.	I must believe my master; else, I promise you,
	I should be arguing still upon that doubt.
	But let it rest, Now, Litio, to you.
	Good master, take it not unkindly, pray,
	That I have been thus pleasant with you both.
Hortensio.	[*To Lucentio*] You may go walk and give me leave a while.
	My lessons make no music in three parts.
Lucentio.	Are you so formal, sir? [*Aside*] Well, I must wait
	And watch withal, for but I be deceived,
	Our fine musician groweth amorous.
Hortensio.	Madam, before you touch the instrument,
	To learn the order of my fingering,
	I must begin with rudiments of art
	To teach you gamut in a briefer sort,
	More pleasant, pithy, and effectual,
	Than hath been taught by any of my trade;
	And there it is in writing, fairly drawn.

Bianca.	Why, I am past my gamut long ago.
Hortensio.	Yet read the gamut of Hortensio.
Bianca.	[*Reads*]

> *Gamut,* I am, the ground of all accord.
>   *A re,* to plead Hortensio's passion:
> *B mi,* Bianca, take him for thy lord,
>   *C fa ut,* that loves with all affection;
> *D sol re,* one clef, two notes have I:
>   *E la mi,* show pity or I die.

Call you this gamut? Tut, I like it not.
Old fashions please me best; I am not so nice
To change true rules for odd inventions.
                [Enter a Messenger]

Messenger.	Mistress, your father prays you leave your books

And help to dress your sister's chamber up.
You know tomorrow is the wedding day.

Bianca.   Farewell, sweet masters both, I must be gone
         [*Exeunt Bianca and Messenger*]
Lucentio.   Faith, mistress, then I have no cause to stay.
         [*Exit*]
Hortensio.   But I have cause to pry into this pedant.
         Methinks he looks as though he were in love.
         Yet if thy thoughts, Bianca, be so humble
         To cast thy wand'ring eyes on every stale,
         Seize thee that list. If once I find thee ranging,
         Hortensio will be quit with thee by changing.
         [*Exit*]

HORTENSIO

[Enter Baptista, Gremio, Tranio as Lucentio, Kate,
Bianca, Lucentio as Cambio and others, Attendants]

Baptista. *[To Tranio]* Signior Lucentio, this is the 'pointed day

That Katherine and Petruchio should be married,

And yet we hear not of our son-in-law.

What will be said? What mockery will it be

To want the bridegroom when the priest attends

To speak the ceremonial rites of marriage!

What says Lucentio to this shame of ours?

Kate. No shame but mine. I must, forsooth, be forced

To give my hand opposed against my heart

Unto a mad-brain rudesby, full of spleen,

Who wooed in haste and means to wed at leisure.

I told you, I, he was a frantic fool,

Hiding his bitter jests in blunt behavior.

And to be noted for a merry man,
He'll woo a thousand, 'point the day of marriage,
Make friends, invite, and proclaim the banns,
Yet never means to wed where he hath wooed.
Now must the world point at poor Katherine
And say, "Lo, there is mad Petruchio's wife,
If it would please him come and marry her."

Tranio. Patience, good Katherine, and Baptista too.
Upon my life, Petruchio means but well,
Whatever fortune stays him from his word.
Though he be blunt, I know him passing wise;
Though he be merry, yet withal he's honest.

Kate. Would Katherine had never seen him though!

[Exit weeping followed by Bianca and others]

Baptista. Go, girl, I cannot blame thee now to weep.
For such an injury would vex a very saint,
Much more a shrew of thy impatient humor.

[Enter Biondello]

Biondello. Master, master, news! And such old news as you never
heard of!

Baptista.	Is it new and old too? How may that be?
Biondello.	Why, is it not news to hear of Petruchio's coming?
Baptista.	Is he come?
Biondello.	Why, no, sir.
Baptista.	What then?
Biondello.	He is coming.
Baptista.	When will he be here?
Biondello.	When he stands where I am and sees you there.
Tranio.	But, say, what to thine old news?
Biondello.	Why, Petruchio is coming in a new hat and an old jerkin; a pair of old breeches thrice turned; a pair of boots that have been candle-cases, one buckled, another laced; an old rusty sword ta'en out of the town armory, with a broken hilt and chapeless; with two broken points; his horse hipped (with an old mothy saddle and stirrups of no kindred), besides, possessed with the glanders and like to mose in the chine; troubled with the lampass, infected with the fashions, full of windgalls, sped

with spavins, rayed with the yellows, past cure of the fives, stark spoiled with the staggers, begnawn with the bots, swayed in the back, and shoulder-shotten; near-legged before, and with a half-cheeked bit and a head-stall of sheep's leather, which, being restrained to keep him from stumbling, hath been often burst and now re-paired with knots; one girth six times pieced, and a wom-an's crupper of velure, which hath two letters for her name fairly set down in studs, and here and there pieced with packthread.

Baptista. Who comes with him?

Biondello. O sir, his lackey, for all the world caparisoned like the horse: with a linen stock on one leg and a kersey boot-hose on the other, gart'red with a red and blue list; an old hat, and the humor of forty fancies pricked in't for a feather—a monster, a very monster in apparel, and not like a Christian footboy or a gentleman's lackey.

Tranio. 'Tis some odd humor pricks him to this fashion,
Yet oftentimes he goes but mean-appareled.

Baptista.	I am glad he's come, howsoe'er he comes.
Biondello.	Why, sir, he comes not.
Baptista.	Didst thou not say he comes?
Biondello.	Who? That Petruchio came?
Baptista.	Ay, that Petruchio came.
Biondello.	No, sir, I say his horse comes, with him on his back.
Baptista.	Why, that's all one.
Biondello.	[*Sings*] Nay, by Saint Jamy,

                                    I hold you a penny,
                                    A horse and a man
                                    Is more than one
                                    And yet not many.

[*Enter Petruchio and Grumio*]

Petruchio.	Come, where be these gallants? Who's at home?
Baptista.	You are welcome, sir.
Petruchio.	And yet I come not well.
Baptista.	And yet you halt not.
Tranio.	Not so well appareled

As I wish you were.

Petruchio. Were it better, I should rush in thus.

But where is Kate? Where is my lovely bride?

How does my father? Gentles, methinks you frown.

And wherefore gaze this goodly company

As if they saw some wondrous monument,

Some comet or unusual prodigy?

Baptista. Why, sir, you know this is your wedding day.

First were we sad, fearing you would not come,

Now sadder that you come so unprovided.

Fie, doff this habit, shame to your estate,

An eyesore to our solemn festival.

Tranio. And tell us what occasion of import

Hath all so long detailed you from your wife

And sent you hither so unlike yourself.

Petruchio. Tedious it were to tell and harsh to hear.

Sufficeth, I am come to keep my word

Though in some part enforcèd to digress,

Which, at more leisure, I will so excuse

As you shall well be satisfied with all.

But where is Kate? I stay too long from her.

The morning wears, 'tis time we were at church.

Tranio.	See not your bride in these unreverent robes.
	Go to my chamber; put on clothes of mine.
Petruchio.	Not I, believe me; thus I'll visit her.
Baptista.	But thus, I trust, you will not marry her.
Petruchio.	Good sooth, even thus; therefore ha' done with words.
	To me she's married, not unto my clothes.
	Could I repair what she will wear in me
	As I can change these poor accoutrements,
	'Twere well for Kate and better for myself.
	But what a fool am I to chat with you
	When I should bid good morrow to my bride
	And seal the title with a lovely kiss.
	[*Exit with Grumio*]
Tranio.	He hath some meaning in his mad attire.
	We will persuade him, be it possible,
	To put on better ere he go to church.

Baptista.   I'll after him and see the event of this.

                  [Exit with Gremio and Attendants]

Tranio.   But to her love concerneth us to add

            Her father's liking, which to bring to pass,

            As I before imparted to your worship,

            I am to get a man—whate'er he be

            It skills not much, we'll fit him to our turn—

            And he shall be Vincentio of Pisa,

            And make assurance here in Padua

            Of greater sums than I have promisèd.

            So shall you quietly enjoy your hope

            And marry sweet Bianca with consent.

Lucentio.   Were it not that my fellow schoolmaster

            Doth watch Bianca's steps so narrowly,

           'Twere good, methinks, to steal our marriage,

            Which once performed, let all the world say no,

            I'll keep mine own despite of all the world.

Tranio. That by degrees we mean to look into
And watch our vantage in this business.
We'll overreach the graybeard, Gremio,
The narrow-prying father, Minola,
The quaint musician, amorous Litio—
All for my master's sake, Lucentio.
  [*Enter Gremio*]
Signior Gremio, came you from the church?

Gremio. As willingly as e'er I came from school.

Tranio. And is the bride and bridegroom coming home?

Gremio. A bridegroom say you? 'Tis a groom indeed,
A grumbling groom, and that the girl shall find.

Tranio. Curster than she? Why, 'tis impossible.

Gremio. Why, he's a devil, a devil, a very fiend.

Tranio. Why, she's a devil, a devil, the devil's dam.

Gremio.	Tut, she's a lamb, a dove, a fool to him.
	I'll tell you, Sir Lucentio, when the priest
	Should ask, if Katherine should be his wife,
	"Ay, by goggs woones!" quoth he and swore so loud
	That, all amazed, the priest let fall the book,
	And as he stooped again to take it up,
	This mad-brained bridegroom took him such a cuff
	That down fell priest and book and book and priest.
	"Now, take them up," quoth he, "if any list."
Tranio.	What said the wench when he rose again?
Gremio.	Trembled and shook, for why he stamped and swore
	As if the vicar meant to cozen him.
	But after many ceremonies done
	He calls for wine. "A health!" quoth he as if
	He had been aboard, carousing to his mates
	After a storm; quaffed off the muscadel
	And threw the sops all in the sexton's face,
	Having no other reason
	But that his beard grew thin and hungerly,

And seemed to ask him sops as he was drinking.

This done, he took the bride about the neck

And kissed her lips with such a clamorous smack

That at the parting all the church did echo,

And I, seeing this, came thence for very shame.

And after me, I know, the rout is coming.

Such a mad marriage never was before.

Hark, hark, I hear the minstrels play.

    [Music plays]

    [Enter Petruchio, Kate, Bianca, Hortensio
    as Litio, Baptista with Grumio and others]

Petruchio.   Gentlemen and friends, I thank you for your pains,

I know you think to dine with me today

And have prepared great store of wedding cheer,

But so it is, my haste doth call me hence

And therefore here I mean to take my leave.

Baptista.   Is't possible you will away tonight?

Petruchio. I must away today, before night come.

Make it no wonder; if you knew my business,

You would entreat me rather go than stay.

And, honest company, I thank you all

That have beheld me give away myself

To this most patient, sweet, and virtuous wife.

Dine with my father, drink a health to me,

For I must hence, and farewell to you all.

Tranio. Let us entreat you stay till after dinner.

Petruchio. It may not be.

Gremio.   Let me entreat you.

Petruchio. It cannot be.

Kate.   Let me entreat you.

Petruchio. I am content.

Kate.   Are you content to stay?

Petruchio. I am content you shall entreat me stay,

But yet not stay, entreat me how you can.

Kate. Now if you love me, stay.

Petruchio.   Grumio, my horse!

Grumio.	Ay, sir, they be ready; the oats have eaten the horses.
Kate.	Nay then,
	Do what thou canst, I will not go today,
	No, nor tomorrow, not till I please myself.
	The door is open, sir, there lies your way.
	You may be jogging whiles your boots are green;
	For me, I'll not be gone till I please myself.
	'Tis like you'll prove a jolly surly groom,
	That take it on you at the first so roundly.
Petruchio.	O Kate, content thee; prithee, be not angry.
Kate.	I will be angry. What hast thou to do?
	Father, be quiet; he shall stay my leisure.
Gremio.	Ay, marry, sir, now it begins to work.
Kate.	Gentlemen, forward to the bridal dinner.
	I see a woman may be made a fool
	If she had not a spirit to resist.
Petruchio.	They shall go forward, Kate, at thy command.
	Obey the bride, you that attend on her.
	Go to the feast, revel and domineer,
	Carouse full measure to her maidenhead,
	Be mad and merry, or go hang yourselves.

But for my bonny Kate, she must with me.

Nay, look not big, nor stamp, nor stare, nor fret;

I will be master of what is mine own.

She is my goods, my chattels; she is my house,

My household stuff, my field, my barn,

My horse, my ox, my ass, my anthing,

And here she stands. Touch her whoever dare,

I'll bring mine action on the proudest he

That stops my way in Padua. Grumio,

Draw forth thy weapon, we are beset with thieves.

Rescue thy mistress, if thou be a man.

Fear not, sweet wench; they shall not touch thee, Kate.

I'll buckler thee against a million.

                [*Exeunt Petruchio, Kate and Grumio*]

Baptista. Nay, let them go, a couple of quiet ones.

Gremio. Went they not quickly, I should die with laughing.

Tranio. Of all mad matches never was the like.

Lucentio. Mistress, what's your opinion of your sister?

Bianca. That being mad herself, she's madly mated.

Gremio.   I warrant him, Petruchio is Kated.

Baptista.   Neighbors and friends, though bride and bridegroom wants
For to supply the places at the table,
You know there wants no junkets at the feast.
[*To Tranio*] Lucentio, you shall supply the bridegroom's place.
And let Bianca take her sister's room.

Tranio.   Shall sweet Bianca practice how to bride it?

Baptista.   She shall, Lucentio. Come, gentlemen, let's go.
[*Exeunt*]

ACT FOUR

PETRUCHIO

SCENE I.
PETRUCHIO'S COUNTRY HOUSE

[Enter Grumio]

Grumio. Fie, fie, on all tired jades, on all mad masters, and all foul ways! Was ever man so beaten? Was ever man so rayed? Was ever man so weary? I am sent before to make a fire, and they are coming after to warm them. Now were not I a little pot and soon hot, my very lips might freeze to my teeth, my tongue to the roof of my mouth, my heart in my belly, ere I should come by a fire to thaw me. But I with blowing the fire shall warm myself, for considering the weather, a taller man than I will take cold. Holla, ho, Curtis!

[Enter Curtis a Servant]

Curtis. Who is that calls so coldly?

Grumio. A piece of ice. If thou doubt it, thou mayst slide from my shoulder to my heel with no greater a run but my head and my neck. A fire, good Curtis.

Curtis. Is my master and his wife coming, Grumio?

Grumio. O ay, Curtis, ay, and therefore fire, fire; cast on no water.

Curtis. Is she so hot a shrew as she's reported?

Grumio. She was, good Curtis, before this frost, but thou know'st winter tames man, woman, and beast; for it hath tamed my old master, and my new mistress, and myself, fellow Curtis.

Curtis. Away, you three-inch fool! I am no beast.

Grumio. Am I but three inches? Why, thy horn is a foot, and so long am I at the least. But wilt thou make a fire, or shall I complain on thee to our mistress, whose hand—she being now at hand—thou shalt soon feel, to thy cold comfort, for being slow in thy hot office?

Curtis. I prithee, good Grumio, tell me, how goes the world?

Grumio. A cold world, Curtis, in every office but thine, and therefore, fire. Do thy duty and have thy duty, for my master and mistress are almost frozen to death.

Curtis. There's fire ready, and therefore, good Grumio, the news.

Grumio. Why, "Jack boy, ho boy!" and as much news as wilt thou.

Curtis. Come, you are so full of cony-catching.

Grumio. Why therefore fire, for I have caught extreme cold. Where's the cook? Is supper ready, the house trimmed, rushes strewed, cobwebs swept, the servingmen in their new fustian, the white stockings, and every officer his wedding garment on? Be the jacks fair within, the jills fair without, the carpets laid and everything in order?

Curtis. All ready, and therefore, I pray thee, news.

Grumio. First, know my horse is tired, my master and mistress fall'n out.

Curtis. How?

Grumio. Out of their saddles into the dirt—and thereby hangs a tale.

Curtis. Let's ha't, good Grumio.

Grumio. Lend thine ear.

Curtis. Here.

Grumio. There.

[Strikes him]

Curtis. This 'tis to feel a tale, not to hear a tale.

Grumio. And therefore 'tis called a sensible tale, and this cuff was but to knock at your ear and beseech list'ning. Now I begin. *Imprimis,* we came down a foul hill, my master riding behind my mistress—

Curtis. Both of one horse?

Grumio. What's that to thee?

Curtis. Why, a horse.

Grumio. Tell thou the tale. But hadst thou not crossed me thou shouldst have heard how her horse fell and she under her horse. Thou shouldst have heard in how miry a place, how she was bemoiled, how he left her with the horse upon her, how he beat me because her horse stumbled, how she waded through the dirt to pluck him off me; how he swore, how she prayed that never prayed before; how I cried, how the horses ran away, how her bridle was burst, how I lost my crupper, with many things of worthy memory which now shall die in oblivion, and thou return unexperienced to thy grave.

Curtis. By this reck'ning he is more shrew than she.

Grumio. Ay, and that thou and the proudest of you all shall find when he comes home. But what talk I of this? Call forth Nathaniel, Joseph, Nicholas, Philip, Walter, Sugarsop, and the rest. Let their heads be slickly combed, their blue coats brushed, and their garters of an indifferent knit. Let them curtsy with their left legs and not presume to touch a hair of my master's horsetail till they kiss their hands. Are they all ready?

Curtis. They are.

Grumio. Call them forth.

Curtis. Do you hear, ho? You must meet my master to countenance my mistress.

Grumio. Why, she hath a face of her own.

Curtis. Who knows not that?

Grumio. Thou, it seems, that calls for company to countenance her.

Curtis. I call them forth to credit her.

Grumio.	Why, she comes to borrow nothing of them.
	[Enter four or five Servingmen]
Nathaniel.	Welcome home, Grumio!
Philip.	How now, Grumio?
Joseph.	What, Grumio!
Nicholas.	Fellow Grumio!
Nathaniel.	How now, old lad!
Grumio.	Welcome, you; how now, you; what, you; fellow, you; and thus much for greeting. Now, my spruce companions, is all ready and all things neat?
Nathaniel.	All things is ready. How near is our master?
Grumio.	E'en at hand, alighted by this, and therfore be not— Cock's passion, silence! I hear my master.
	[Enter Petruchio and Kate]
Petruchio.	Where be these knaves? What, no man at door To hold my stirrup nor to take my horse? Where is Nathaniel, Gregory, Philip?
All Servingmen.	Here, here, sir, here, sir.

Petruchio. Here, sir, here, sir, here, sir, here, sir!

You loggerheaded and unpolished grooms!

What, no attendance? No regard? No duty?

Where is the foolish knave I sent before?

Grumio. Here, sir, as foolish as I was before.

Petruchio. You peasant swain! You whoreson malt-horse drudge!

Did I not bid thee meet me in the park

And bring along these rascal knaves with thee?

Grumio. Nathaniel's coat, sir, was not fully made

And Gabrel's pumps were all unpinked i' th' heel.

There was no link to color Peter's hat,

And Walter's dagger was not come from sheathing.

There were none fine but Adam, Rafe, and Gregory;

The rest were ragged, old, and beggarly.

Yet, as they are, here are they come to meet you.

Petruchio.   Go, rascals, go, and fetch my supper in.

     [Exeunt Servants]

[Sings]   "Where is the life that late I led?"

Where are those—Sit down, Kate, and welcome.

Soud, soud, soud, soud!

     [Enter Servants with supper]

Why, when, I say?—Nay, good sweet Kate, be merry.—

Off with my boots, you rogues, you villains! When?

[Sings]   "It was the friar of orders gray,
          As he forth walkèd on his way"—

Out, you rogue, you pluck my foot awry!

Take that, and mend the plucking of the other.

     [Strikes him]

Be merry, Kate. Some water here! What ho!

     [Enter one with water]

Where's my spaniel Troilus? Sirrah, get you hence

And bid my cousin Ferdinand come hither —

     [Exit Servant]

One, Kate, that you must kiss and be acquainted with.

Where are my slippers? Shall I have some water?

Come, Kate, and wash, and welcome heartily.

You whoreson villain, will you let it fall?

    [Strikes him]

Kate. Patience, I pray you. 'Twas a fault unwilling.

Petruchio. A whoreson, beetle-headed, flap-eared knave!

Come, Kate, sit down; I know you have a stomach.

Will you give thanks, sweet Kate, or else shall I?

What's this? Mutton?

First Servingman.   Ay.

Petruchio.   Who brought it?

Peter.   I.

Petruchio. 'Tis burnt, and so is all the meat.

What dogs are these! Where is the rascal cook?

How durst you, villains, bring it from the dresser,

And serve it thus to me that love it not?

There, take it to you, trenchers, cups, and all,

    [Throws food and dishes at them]

You heedless joltheads and unmannered slaves!

What, do you grumble? I'll be with you straight.

Kate.	I pray you, husband, be not so disquiet.
	The meat was well if you were so contented.
Petruchio.	I tell thee, Kate, 'twas burnt and dried away,
	And I expressly am forbid to touch it,
	For it engenders choler, planteth anger,
	And better 'twere that both of us did fast—
	Since of ourselves, ourselves are choleric—
	Than feed it with such overroasted flesh.
	Be patient. Tomorrow't shall be mended,
	And for this night we'll fast for company.
	Come, I will bring thee to thy bridal chamber.
	[Exeunt. Enter servants severally]
Nathaniel.	Peter, didst ever see the like?
Peter.	He kills her in her own humor.
	[Enter Curtis, a Servant]
Grumio.	Where is he?

Curtis.   In her chamber, making a sermon of continency to her,
And rails and swears and rates, that she, poor soul,
Knows not which way to stand, to look, to speak,
And sits as one new-risen from a dream.
Away, away, for he is coming hither.
    [*Exeunt. Enter Petruchio*]
Petruchio.   Thus have I politicly begun my reign,
And 'tis my hope to end successfully.
My falcon now is sharp and passing empty,
And till she stoop she must not be full gorged,
For then she never looks upon her lure.
Another way I have to man my haggard,
To make her come and know her keeper's call,
That is, to watch her as we watch these kites
That bate and beat and will not be obedient.
She eat no meat today, nor none shall eat.
Last night she slept not, nor tonight she shall not.

As with the meat, some undeservèd fault

I'll find about the making of the bed,

And here I'll fling the pillow, there the bolster,

This way the coverlet, another way the sheets.

Ay, and amid this hurly I intend

That all is done in reverent care of her,

And in conclusion she shall watch all night.

And if she chance to nod I'll rail and brawl

And with the clamor keep her still awake.

This is a way to kill a wife with kindness,

And thus I'll curb her mad and headstrong humor.

He that knows better how to tame a shrew,

Now let him speak—'tis charity to show.

    [Exit]

[*Enter Tranio as Lucentio and Hortensio as Litio*]

Tranio. Is't possible, friend Litio, that Mistress Bianca
Doth fancy any other but Lucentio?
I tell you, sir, she bears me fair in hand.

Hortensio. Sir, to satisfy you in what I have said,
Stand by and mark the manner of his teaching.

[*They eavesdrop. Enter Bianca, Lucentio as Cambio*]

Lucentio. Now mistress, profit you in what you read?

Bianca. What, master, read you? First resolve me that.

Lucentio. I read that I profess, the Art to Love.

Bianca. And may you prove, sir, master of your art.

Lucentio. While you, sweet dear, prove mistress of my heart.

[*They court*]

Hortensio. Quick proceeders, marry! Now, tell me, I pray,
You that durst swear that your mistress Bianca
Loved none in the world so well as Lucentio.

Tranio.	O despiteful love! Unconstant womankind!
	I tell thee, Litio, this is wonderful.
Hortensio.	Mistake no more. I am not Litio,
	Nor a musician, as I seem to be,
	But one that scorn to live in this disguise,
	For such a one as leaves a gentleman
	And makes a god of such a cullion.
	Know, sir, that I am called Hortensio.
Tranio.	Signior Hortensio, I have often heard
	Of your entire affection to Bianca,
	And since mine eyes are witness of her lightness,
	I will with you, if you be so contented,
	Forswear Bianca and her love forever.
Hortensio.	See, how they kiss and court! Signior Lucentio,
	Here is my hand and here I firmly vow
	Never to woo her more, but do forswear her,
	As one unworthy all the former favors
	That I have fondly flattered her withal.

Tranio. And here I take the like unfeignèd oath,

Never to marry with her though she would entreat.

Fie on her! See how beastly she doth court him.

Hortensio. Would all the world but he had quite forsworn.

For me, that I may surely keep mine oath,

I will be married to a wealthy widow

Ere three days pass, which hath as long loved me

As I have loved this proud disdainful haggard.

And so farewell, Signior Lucentio.

Kindness in women, not their beauteous looks,

Shall win my love, and so I take my leave

In resolution as I swore before.

  [Exit]

Tranio. Mistress Bianca, bless you with such grace

As 'longeth to a lover's blessèd case.

Nay, I have ta'en you napping, gentle love,

And have forsworn you with Hortensio.

Bianca. Tranio, you jest. But have you both forsworn me?

Tranio.	Mistress, we have.
Lucentio.	Then we are rid of Litio.
Tranio.	I' faith, he'll have a lusty widow now,
	That shall be wooed and wedded in a day.
Bianca.	God give him joy!
Tranio.	Ay, and he'll tame her.
Bianca.	He says so, Tranio.
Tranio.	Faith, he is gone unto the taming school.
Bianca.	The taming school! What, is there such a place?
Tranio.	Ay, mistress, and Petruchio is the master,
	That teacheth tricks eleven and twenty long
	To tame a shrew and charm her chattering tongue.
	[*Enter Biondello*]
Biondello.	O master, master, I have watched so long
	That I am dog-weary, but at last I spied
	An ancient angel coming down the hill
	Will serve the turn.
Tranio.	What is he, Biondello?

Biondello.	Master, a mercatante or a pedant,
	I know not what, but formal in apparel,
	In gait and countenance surely like a father.
Lucentio.	And what of him, Tranio?
Tranio.	If he be credulous and trust my tale,
	I'll make him glad to seem Vincentio,
	And give assurance to Baptista Minola
	As if he were the right Vincentio.
	Take in your love and then let me alone.

[Exeunt Lucentio and Bianca. Enter a Pedant]

Pedant.	God save you, sir.
Tranio.	And you, sir. You are welcome.
	Travel you far on, or are you at the farthest?
Pedant.	Sir, at the farthest for a week or two,
	But then up farther and as far as Rome,
	And so to Tripoli if God lend me life.
Tranio.	What countryman, I pray?
Pedant.	Of Mantua.

Tranio.	Of Mantua, sir? Marry, God forbid!
	And come to Padua, careless of your life?
Pedant.	My life, sir? How, I pray? For that goes hard.
Tranio.	'Tis death for anyone in Mantua
	To come to Padua. Know you not the cause?
	Your ships are stayed at Venice and the Duke,
	For private quarrel 'twixt your duke and him,
	Hath published and proclaimed it openly.
	'Tis marvel, but that you are but newly come,
	You might have heard it else proclaimed about.
Pedant.	Alas, sir, it is worse for me than so,
	For I have bills for money by exchange
	From Florence and must here deliver them.
Tranio.	Well, sir, to do you courtesy,
	This will I do and this I will advise you.
	First tell me, have you ever been at Pisa?
Pedant.	Ay, sir, in Pisa have I often been—
	Pisa, renownèd for grave citizens.
Tranio.	Among them, know you one Vincentio?

Pedant.	I know him not but I have heard of him—
	A merchant of incomparable wealth.
Tranio.	He is my father, sir, and, sooth to say,
	In count'nance somewhat doth resemble you.
Biondello.	[Aside] As much as an apple doth an oyster, and all one.
Tranio.	To save your life in this extremity,
	This favor will I do you for his sake,
	And think it not the worst of all your fortunes
	That you are like to Sir Vincentio.
	His name and credit shall you undertake,
	And in my house you shall be friendly lodged.
	Look that you take upon you as you should.
	You understand me, sir? So shall you stay
	Till you have done your business in the city.
	If this be court'sy, sir, accept of it.
Pedant.	O sir, I do, and will repute you ever
	The patron of my life and liberty.

Tranio.   Then go with me to make the matter good.
This, by the way, I let you understand:
My father is here looked for every day
To pass assurance of a dower in marriage
'Twixt me and one Baptista's daughter here.
In all these circumstances I'll instruct you.
Go with me to clothe you as becomes you.

    [Exeunt]

KATE

[Enter Kate and Grumio]

Grumio. No, no, forsooth, I dare not for my life.

Kate. The more my wrong, the more his spite appears.

What, did he marry me to famish me?

Beggars that come unto my father's door,

Upon entreaty have a present alms;

If not, elsewhere they meet with charity.

But I, who never knew how to entreat

Nor never needed that I should entreat,

Am starved for meat, giddy for lack of sleep,

With oaths kept waking and with brawling fed.

And that which spites me more than all these wants,

He does it under name of perfect love,

As who should say, if I should sleep or eat

'Twere deadly sickness or else present death.

I prithee go and get me some repast,

I care not what, so it be wholesome food.

Grumio.	What say you to a neat's foot?
Kate.	'Tis passing good; I prithee let me have it.
Grumio.	I fear it is too choleric a meat.
	How say you to a fat tripe finely broiled?
Kate.	I like it well. Good Grumio, fetch it me.
Grumio.	I cannot tell, I fear 'tis choleric.
	What say you to a piece of beef and mustard?
Kate.	A dish that I do love to feed upon.
Grumio.	Ay, but the mustard is too hot a little.
Kate.	Why then, the beef, and let the mustard rest.
Grumio.	Nay then, I will not. You shall have the mustard
	Or else you get no beef of Grumio.
Kate.	Then both or one, or anything thou wilt.
Grumio.	Why then, the mustard without the beef.
Kate.	Go, get thee gone, thou false deluding slave,
	[*Beats him*]
	That feed'st me with the very name of meat.
	Sorrow on thee and all the pack of you
	That triumph thus upon my misery.
	Go, get thee gone, I say.

[Enter Petruchio and Hortensio with meat]

Petruchio. How fares my Kate? What, sweeting, all amort?

Hortensio. Mistress, what cheer?

Kate.   Faith, as cold as can be.

Petruchio. Pluck up thy spirits; look cheerfully upon me.
Here, love, thou seest how diligent I am
To dress thy meat myself and bring it thee.
I am sure, sweet Kate, this kindness merits thanks.
What, not a word? Nay then, thou lov'st it not,
And all my pains is sorted to no proof.
Here, take away this dish.

Kate.   I pray you, let it stand.

Petruchio. The poorest service is repaid with thanks,
And so shall mine before you touch the meat.

Kate. I thank you, sir.

Hortensio. Signior Petruchio, fie, you are to blame.
Come, Mistress Kate, I'll bear you company.

Petruchio. [*Aside*] Eat it up all, Hortensio, if thou lovest me;

Much good do it unto thy gentle heart.

Kate, eat apace. And now, my honey love,

Will we return unto thy father's house

And revel it as bravely as the best,

With silken coats and caps and golden rings,

With ruffs and cuffs and fardingales and things,

With scarfs and fans and double change of brav'ry,

With amber bracelets, beads, and all this knav'ry.

What, hast thou dined? The tailor stays thy leisure

To deck thy body with his ruffling treasure.

    [*Enter Tailor*]

Come, tailor, let us see these ornaments.

    [*Enter Haberdasher*]

Lay forth the gown. What news with you, sir?

Haberdasher. Here is the cap your Worship did bespeak.

Petruchio. Why, this was molded on a porringer—
A velvet dish. Fie, fie, 'tis lewd and filthy.
Why, 'tis a cockle or a walnut shell,
A knack, a toy, a trick, a baby's cap.
Away with it! Come, let me have a bigger.

Kate. I'll have no bigger. This doth fit the time,
And gentlewomen wear such caps as these.

Petruchio. When you are gentle you shall have one too.
And not till then.

Hortensio. [*Aside*] That will not be in haste.

Kate. Why, sir, I trust I may have leave to speak,
And speak I will. I am no child, no babe.
Your betters have endured me say my mind,
And if you cannot, best you stop your ears.
My tongue will tell the anger of my heart,
Or else my heart, concealing it, will break,
And rather than it shall I will be free
Even to the uttermost, as I please, in words.

Petruchio.   Why, thou sayst true. It is a paltry cap,

           A custard-coffin, a bauble, a silken pie.

           I love thee well in that thou lik'st it not.

Kate.   Love me or love me not, I like the cap,

           And it I will have or I will have none.

              [Exit Haberdasher]

Petruchio.   Thy gown? Why, ay. Come, tailor, let us see't.

           O mercy, God! What masquing stuff is here?

           What's this? A sleeve? 'Tis like a demi-cannon.

           What, up and down, carved like an apple tart?

           Here's snip and nip and cut and slish and slash,

           Like to a censer in a barber's shop.

           Why, what, a devil's name, tailor, call'st thou this?

Hortensio.   *[Aside]* I see she's like to have neither cap nor gown.

Tailor.   You bid me make it orderly and well,

           According to the fashion and the time.

Petruchio.	Marry, and did, but if you be rememb'red,
	I did not bid you mar it to the time.
	Go, hop me over every kennel home,
	For you shall hop without my custom, sir.
	I'll none of it. Hence, make your best of it.
Kate.	I never saw a better-fashioned gown,
	More quaint, more pleasing, nor more commendable.
	Belike you mean to make a puppet of me.
Petruchio.	Why, true, he means to make a puppet of thee.
Tailor.	She says your worship means to make a puppet of her.
Petruchio.	O monstrous arrogance!
	Thou liest, thou thread, thou thimble,
	Thou yard, three-quarters, half-yard, quarter, nail!
	Thou flea, thou nit, thou winter cricket thou!
	Braved in mine own house with a skein of thread!
	Away, thou rag, thou quantity, thou remnant,
	Or I shall so bemete thee with thy yard
	As thou shalt think on prating whilst thou liv'st.
	I tell thee, I, that thou hast marred her gown.

Tailor.	Your worship is deceived. The gown is made
	Just as my master had direction.
	Grumio gave order how it should be done.
Grumio.	I gave him no order; I gave him the stuff.
Tailor.	But how did you desire it should be made?
Grumio.	Marry, sir, with needle and thread.
Tailor.	But did you not request to have it cut?
Grumio.	Thou hast faced many things.
Tailor.	I have.
Grumio.	Face not me. Thou hast braved many men; brave not me.
	I will neither be faced nor braved. I say unto thee, I bid
	thy master cut out the gown, but I did not bid him cut it
	to pieces. *Ergo,* thou liest.
Tailor.	Why, here is the note of the fashion to testify.
Petruchio.	Read it.
Grumio.	The note lies in's throat if he say I said so.
Tailor.	"*Imprimis,* a loose-bodied gown."

Grumio. Master, if ever I said loose-bodied gown, sew me in the skirts of it and beat me to death with a bottom of brown thread. I said, a gown.

Petruchio. Proceed.

Tailor. "With a small compassed cape."

Grumio. I confess the cape.

Tailor. "With a trunk sleeve."

Grumio. I confess two sleeves.

Tailor. "The sleeves curiously cut."

Petruchio. Ay, there's the villainy.

Grumio. Error i' th' bill, sir, error i' th' bill. I commanded the sleeves should be cut out and sewed up again, and that I'll prove upon thee, though thy little finger be armed in a thimble.

Tailor. This is true that I say. And I had thee in place where, thou shouldst know it.

Grumio. I am for thee straight. Take thou the bill, give me thy mete-yard, and spare not me.

Hortensio.	God-a-mercy, Grumio, then he shall have no odds.
Petruchio.	Well, sir, in brief, the gown is not for me.
Grumio.	You are i' th' right, sir; 'tis for my mistress.
Petruchio.	Go, take it up unto thy master's use.
Grumio.	Villain, not for thy life! Take up my mistress' gown for thy master's use!
Petruchio.	Why sir, what's your conceit in that?
Grumio.	O sir, the conceit is deeper than you think for. Take up my mistress' gown to his master's use! O, fie, fie, fie!
Petruchio.	[*Aside*] Hortensio, say thou wilt see the tailor paid. [*To Tailor*] Go take it hence; be gone and say no more.
Hortensio.	Tailor, I'll pay thee for thy gown tomorrow; Take no unkindness of his hasty words. Away, I say, commend me to thy master.

       [Exit Tailor]

Petruchio. Well, come, my Kate, we will unto your father's,
Even in these honest mean habiliments.
Our purses shall be proud, our garments poor,
For 'tis the mind that makes the body rich,
And as the sun breaks through the darkest clouds
So honor peereth in the meanest habit.
What, is the jay more precious than the lark
Because his feathers are more beautiful?
Or is the adder better than the eel
Because his painted skin contents the eye?
O no, good Kate, neither art thou the worse
For this poor furniture and mean array.
If thou account'st it shame, lay it on me,
And therefore frolic. We will hence forthwith
To feast and sport us at thy father's house.
[*To Grumio*] Go call my men, and let us straight to him;
And bring our horses unto Long-lane end.
There will we mount, and thither walk on foot.
Let's see, I think 'tis now some seven o'clock,
And well we may come there by dinnertime.

Kate. I dare assure you, sir, 'tis almost two,
And 'twill be suppertime ere you come there.

Petruchio. It shall be seven ere I go to horse.
Look what I speak or do or think to do,
You are still crossing it. Sirs, let't alone:
I will not go today, and ere I do,
It shall be what o'clock I say it is.

Hortensio. [Aside] Why, so this gallant will command the sun.
[Exeunt]

[Enter Tranio as Lucentio and
Pedant dressed like Vincentio]

Tranio. Sir, this is the house. Please it you that I call?

Pedant. Ay, what else? And but I be deceived,
Signior Baptista may remember me
Near twenty years ago in Genoa,
Where we were lodgers at the Pegasus.

Tranio. 'Tis well, and hold your own in any case
With such austerity as 'longeth to a father.

Pedant. I warrant you. But sir, here comes your boy;
'Twere good he were schooled.

[Enter Biondello]

Tranio. Fear you not him. Sirrah Biondello,
Now do your duty throughly, I advise you.
Imagine 'twere the right Vincentio.

Biondello. Tut, fear not me.

Tranio. But hast thou done thy errand to Baptista?

Biondello. I told him that your father was at Venice
          And that you looked for him this day in Padua.
Tranio. Th' art a tall fellow. Hold thee that to drink.
          Here comes Baptista. Set your countenance, sir.
              [*Enter Baptista and Lucentio as Cambio*
              with the Pedant booted and bareheaded]
          Signior Baptista, you are happily met.
          [*To the Pedant*] Sir, this is the gentleman I told you of.
          I pray you, stand good father to me now,
          Give me Bianca for my patrimony.
Pedant. Soft, son.
          Sir, by your leave. Having come to Padua
          To gather in some debts, my son Lucentio
          Made me acquainted with a weighty cause
          Of love between your daughter and himself.
          And—for the good report I hear of you,
          And for the love he beareth to your daughter,
          And she to him—to stay him not too long,

I am content, in a good father's care,

To have him matched. And if you please to like

No worse than I, upon some agreement

Me shall you find ready and willing

With one consent to have her so bestowed,

For curious I cannot be with you,

Signior Baptista, of whom I hear so well.

Baptista. Sir, pardon me in what I have to say.

Your plainness and your shortness please me well.

Right true it is, your son Lucentio here

Doth love my daughter and she loveth him—

Or both dissemble deeply their affections—

And therefore, if you say no more than this,

That like a father you will deal with him

And pass my daughter a sufficient dower,

The match is made, and all is done.

Your son shall have my daughter with consent.

Tranio. I thank you, sir. Where, then, do you know best

We be affied and such assurance ta'en

As shall with either part's agreement stand?

Baptista.	Not in my house, Lucentio, for you know
	Pitchers have ears, and I have many servants.
	Besides, old Gremio is heark'ning still,
	And happily we might be interrupted.
Tranio.	Then at my lodging and it like you.
	There doth my father lie, and there this night
	We'll pass the business privately and well.
	Send for your daughter by your servant here;
	My boy shall fetch the scrivener presently.
	The worst is this, that at so slender warning
	You are like to have a thin and slender pittance.
Baptista.	It likes me well. Cambio, hie you home
	And bid Bianca make her ready straight,
	And, if you will, tell what hath happenèd:
	Lucentio's father is arrived in Padua,
	And how she's like to be Lucentio's wife.
	[*Exit Lucentio*]
Biondello.	I pray the gods she may with all my heart!
	[*Exit*]

Tranio.	Dally not with the gods, but get thee gone.
	Signior Baptista, shall I lead the way?
	Welcome, one mess is like to be your cheer.
	Come, sir, we will better it in Pisa.
Baptista.	I follow you.

[*Exeunt. Enter Lucentio as Cambio and Biondello*]

Biondello.	Cambio!
Lucentio.	What sayst thou, Biondello?
Biondello.	You saw my master wink and laugh upon you?
Lucentio.	Biondello, what of that?
Biondello.	Faith, nothing, but has left me here behind to expound the meaning or moral of his signs and tokens.
Lucentio.	I pray thee, moralize them.
Biondello.	Then thus. Baptista is safe, talking with the deceiving father of a deceitful son.
Lucentio.	And what of him?
Biondello.	His daughter is to be brought by you to the supper.
Lucentio.	And then?

Biondello. The old priest at Saint Luke's church is at your command at all hours.

Lucentio. And what of all this?

Biondello. I cannot tell, except they are busied about a counterfeit assurance. Take you assurance of her, *"cum previlegio ad impremendum solem."* To th' church! Take the priest, clerk, and some sufficient honest witnesses.

If this be not that you look for, I have no more to say,
But bid Bianca farewell forever and a day.

Lucentio. Hear'st thou, Biondello?

Biondello. I cannot tarry. I knew a wench married in an afternoon as she went to the garden for parsley to stuff a rabbit. And so may you, sir. And so adieu, sir. My master hath appointed me to go to Saint Luke's, to bid the priest be ready to come against you come with your appendix.

Lucentio. I may, and will, if she be so contented.

　　　[*Exit*]

She will be pleased; then wherefore should I doubt?
Hap what hap may, I'll roundly go about her.
It shall go hard if Cambio go without her.

　　　[*Exit*]

[Enter Petruchio, Kate, Hortensio with Servants]

Petruchio.   Come on, a God's name, once more toward our father's.

            Good Lord, how bright and goodly shines the moon.

Kate.   The moon? The sun. It is not moonlight now.

Petruchio.   I say it is the moon that shines so bright.

Kate.   I know it is the sun that shines so bright.

Petruchio.   Now, by my mother's son, and that's myself,

            It shall be moon or star or what I list,

            Or ere I journey to your father's house.

            [To Servants] Go on and fetch our horses back again.

            Evermore crossed and crossed, nothing but crossed!

Hortensio.   *[To Kate]* Say as he says or we shall never go.

Kate.   Forward, I pray, since we have come so far,

            And be it moon or sun or what you please.

            And if you please to call it a rush-candle,

            Henceforth I vow it shall be so for me.

Petruchio.	I say it is the moon.
Kate.	I know it is the moon.
Petruchio.	Nay, then you lie. It is the blessèd sun.
Kate.	Then God be blessed, it is the blessèd sun.
	But sun it is not, when you say it is not,
	And the moon changes even as your mind.
	What you will have it named, even that it is,
	And so it shall be so for Katherine.
Hortensio.	[*Aside*] Petruchio, go thy ways. The field is won.
Petruchio.	Well, forward, forward! Thus the bowl should run
	And not unluckily against the bias.
	But soft, company is coming here.

    [*Enter Vincentio*]

[*To Vincentio*] Good morrow, gentle mistress; where away?
Tell me, sweet Kate, and tell me truly too,
Hast thou beheld a fresher gentlewoman?
Such war of white and red within her cheeks!
What stars do spangle heaven with such beauty
As those two eyes become that heavenly face?
Fair lovely maid, once more good day to thee.
Sweet Kate, embrace her for her beauty's sake.

Hortensio.	[*Aside*] 'A will make the man mad, to make a woman of him.
Kate.	Young budding virgin, fair and fresh and sweet,
	Whither away, or where is thy abode?
	Happy the parents of so fair a child!
	Happier the man whom favorable stars
	Allots thee for his lovely bedfellow!
Petruchio.	Why, how now, Kate, I hope thou are not mad.
	This is a man, old, wrinkled, faded, withered,
	And not a maiden, as thou sayst he is.
Kate.	Pardon, old father, my mistaking eyes
	That have been so bedazzled with the sun
	That everything I look on seemeth green.
	Now I perceive thou art a reverend father;
	Pardon, I pray thee, for my mad mistaking.
Petruchio.	Do, good old grandsire, and withal make known
	Which way thou travelest. If along with us,
	We shall be joyful of thy company.

Vincentio. Fair sir, and you my merry mistress,
That with your strange encounter much amazed me,
My name is called Vincentio, my dwelling Pisa,
And bound I am to Padua, there to visit
A son of mine which long I have not seen.

Petruchio. What is his name?

Vincentio.   Lucentio, gentle sir.

Petruchio. Happily met, the happier for thy son.
And now by law as well as reverend age,
I may entitle thee my loving father.
The sister to my wife, this gentlewoman,
Thy son by this hath married. Wonder not
Nor be not grieved. She is of good esteem,
Her dowry wealthy, and of worthy birth;
Beside, so qualified as may beseem
The spouse of any noble gentleman.
Let me embrace with old Vincentio
And wander we to see thy honest son,
Who will of thy arrival be full joyous.

Vincentio.	But is this true, or is it else your pleasure,
	Like pleasant travelers, to break a jest
	Upon the company you overtake?
Hortensio.	I do assure thee, father, so it is.
Petruchio.	Come, go along, and see the truth hereof,
	For our first merriment hath made thee jealous.

      [Exeunt all but Hortensio]

Hortensio.	Well, Petruchio, this has put me in heart.
	Have to my widow, and if she be froward,
	Then hast thou taught Hortensio to be untoward.

      [Exit]

ACT FIVE

VINCENTIO

SCENE I

PADUA IN FRONT OF LUCENTIO'S HOUSE

[Enter Biondello, Lucentio as Cam-
bio and Bianca; Gremio is out before]

Biondello. Softly and swiftly, sir, for the priest is ready.

Lucentio. I fly, Biondello. But they may chance to need thee at
home; therefore leave us.

  [Exit with Bianca]

Biondello. Nay, faith, I'll see the church a your back, and then
come back to my master's as soon as I can.

  [Exit]

Gremio. I marvel Cambio comes not all this while.

  [Enter Petruchio, Grumio, Vincentio,
  and Kate, along with Attendants]

Petruchio. Sir, here's the door, this is Lucentio's house.
My father's bears more toward the marketplace;
Thither must I, and here I leave you, sir.

Vincentio. You shall not choose but drink before you go.
I think I shall command your welcome here,
And by all likelihood some cheer is toward. *[Knock]*

Gremio. They're busy within. You were best knock louder.

*[Pedant, as Vincentio, looks
out of the window above]*

Pedant. What's he that knocks as he would beat down the gate?

Vincentio. Is Signior Lucentio within, sir?

Pedant. He's within, sir, but not to be spoken withal.

Vincentio. What if a man bring him a hundred pound or two, to make merry withal?

Pedant. Keep your hundred pounds to yourself; he shall need none so long as I live.

Petruchio. Nay, I told you your son was well beloved in Padua. Do you hear, sir? To leave frivolous circumstances, I pray you tell Signior Lucentio that his father is come from Pisa and is here at the door to speak with him.

Pedant. Thou liest. His father is come from Padua and here looking out at the window.

Vincentio. Art thou his father?

Pedant. Ay sir, so his mother says, if I may believe her.

Petruchio. [*To Vincentio*] Why how now, gentleman? Why this is flat knavery, to take upon you another man's name.

Pedant. Lay hands on the villain. I believe 'a means to cozen somebody in this city under my countenance.

[*Enter Biondello*]

Biondello. I have seen them in the church together; God send 'em good shipping! But who is here? Mine old master, Vincentio! Now we are undone and brought to nothing.

Vincentio. Come hither, crack-hemp.

Biondello. I hope I may choose, sir.

Vincentio. Come hither, you rogue. What, have you forgot me?

Biondello. Forgot you? No, sir. I could not forget you, for I never saw you before in all my life.

Vincentio. What, you notorious villain, didst thou never see thy master's father, Vincentio?

Biondello. What, my old worshipful old master? Yes, marry, sir, see where he looks out of the window.

Vincentio.	Is't so, indeed?
	[*He beats Biondello*]
Biondello.	Help, help, help! Here's a madman will murder me.
	[*Exit*]
Pedant.	Help, son! Help, Signior Baptista!
	[*Exit from above*]
Petruchio.	Prithee, Kate, let's stand aside and see the end of this controversy.
	[*They stand aside*]
	[*Enter Pedant below with Servants, Baptista, and Tranio as Lucentio*]
Tranio.	Sir, what are you that offer to beat my servant?
Vincentio.	What am I, sir? Nay, what are you, sir? O immortal gods! O fine villain! A silken doublet, a velvet hose, a scarlet cloak, and a copatain hat! O, I am undone, I am undone! While I play the good husband at home, my son and my servant spend all at the university.
Tranio.	How now, what's the matter?
Baptista.	What, is the man lunatic?

Tranio. Sir, you seem a sober ancient gentleman by your habit, but your words show you a madman. Why sir, what 'cerns it you if I wear pearl or gold? I thank my good father, I am able to maintain it.

Vincentio. Thy father! O villain, he is a sailmaker in Bergamo.

Baptista. You mistake, sir, you mistake, sir. Pray, what do you think is his name?

Vincentio. His name! As if I knew not his name! I have brought him up ever since he was three years old, and his name is Tranio.

Pedant. Away, away, mad ass! His name is Lucentio, and he is mine only son and heir to the lands of me, Signior Vincentio.

Vincentio. Lucentio! O he hath murd'red his master. Lay hold on him, I charge you in the Duke's name. O my son, my son! Tell me, thou villain, where is my son Lucentio?

Tranio. Call forth an officer.

[Enter an Officer]

Carry this mad knave to the jail. Father Baptista, I charge you see that he be forthcoming.

Vincentio.	Carry me to the jail!
Gremio.	Stay, officer. He shall not go to prison.
Baptista.	Talk not, Signior Gremio. I say he shall go to prison.
Gremio.	Take heed, Signior Baptista, lest you be cony-catched in this business. I dare swear this is the right Vincentio.
Pedant.	Swear, if thou dar'st.
Gremio.	Nay, I dare not swear it.
Tranio.	Then thou wert best say that I am not Lucentio.
Gremio.	Yes, I know thee to be Signior Lucentio.
Baptista.	Away with the dotard, to the jail with him!
Vincentio.	Thus strangers may be haled and abused. O monstrous villain!

[Enter Biondello, Lucentio, and Bianca]

Biondello.	O we are spoiled—and yonder he is. Deny him, forswear him, or else we are all undone.

[Exit Biondello, Tranio, and Pedant as fast as may be]

Lucentio.	Pardon, sweet father.

[Kneel]

Vincentio.	Lives my sweet son?

Bianca.	Pardon, dear father.
Baptista.	How hast thou offended?
	Where is Lucentio?
Lucentio.	Here's Lucentio,
	Right son to the right Vincentio,
	That have by marriage made thy daughter mine
	While counterfeit supposes bleared thine eyne.
Gremio.	Here's packing, with a witness, to deceive us all!
Vincentio.	Where is that damnèd villain Tranio
	That faced and braved me in this matter so?
Baptista.	Why, tell me, is not this my Cambio?
Bianca.	Cambio is changed into Lucentio.
Lucentio.	Love wrought these miracles. Bianca's love
	Made me exchange my state with Tranio
	While he did bear my countenance in the town,
	And happily I have arrived at the last
	Unto the wishèd haven of my bliss.
	What Tranio did, myself enforced him to.
	Then pardon him, sweet father, for my sake.
Vincentio.	I'll slit the villain's nose that would have sent me to the jail.

Baptista. [*To Lucentio*] But do you hear, sir? Have you married my daughter without asking my good will?

Vincentio. Fear not, Baptista; we will content you, go to. But I will in, to be revenged for this villainy.

[*Exit*]

Baptista. And I, to sound the depth of this knavery.

[*Exit*]

Lucentio. Look not pale, Bianca. Thy father will not frown.

[*Exeunt Lucentio and Bianca*]

Gremio. My cake is dough, but I'll in among the rest
Out of hope of all but my share of the feast.

[*Exit*]

Kate. Husband, let's follow, to see the end of this ado.

Petruchio. First kiss me, Kate, and we will.

Kate. What, in the midst of the street?

Petruchio. What, art thou ashamed of me?

Kate. No sir, God forbid, but ashamed to kiss.

Petruchio.   Why, then let's home again.

             [*To Grumio*] Come sirrah, let's away.

Kate.   Nay, I will give thee a kiss. Now pray thee, love, stay.

Petruchio.   Is not this well? Come, my sweet Kate.

             Better once than never, for never too late.

             [*Exeunt*]

SCENE II

PADUA. IN LUCENTIO'S HOUSE

[*Enter Baptista, Vincentio, Gremio, the Pedant,
Lucentio, and Bianca, Petruchio, Kate, Hortensio,
Tranio, Biondello, Grumio, and the Widow; the
Servingmen with Tranio bringing in a banquet*]

Lucentio.   At last, though long, our jarring notes agree,

And time it is, when raging war is done,

To smile at 'scapes and perils overblown.

My fair Bianca, bid my father welcome

While I with self-same kindness welcome thine.

Brother Petruchio, sister Katherina,

And thou, Hortensio, with thy loving widow,

Feast with the best and welcome to my house.

My banquet is to close our stomachs up

After our great good cheer. Pray you, sit down,

For now we sit to chat as well as eat.

Petruchio.   Nothing but sit and sit, and eat and eat.

Baptista.   Padua affords this kindness, son Petruchio.

Petruchio.	Padua affords nothing but what is kind.
Hortensio.	For both our sakes I would that word were true.
Petruchio.	Now, for my life, Hortensio fears his widow.
Widow.	Then never trust me if I be afeard.
Petruchio.	You are very sensible and yet you miss my sense:
	I mean Hortensio is afeard of you.
Widow.	He that is giddy thinks the world turns round.
Petruchio.	Roundly replied.
Kate.	Mistress, how mean you that?
Widow.	Thus I conceive by him.
Petruchio.	Conceives by me! How likes Hortensio that?
Hortensio.	My widow says, thus she conceives her tale.
Petruchio.	Very well mended. Kiss him for that, good widow.
Kate.	"He that is giddy thinks the world turns round."
	I pray you, tell me what you meant by that.
Widow.	Your husband, being troubled with a shrew,
	Measures my husband's sorrow by his woe,
	And now you know my meaning.

Kate.	A very mean meaning.
Widow.	Right, I mean you.
Kate.	And I am mean indeed, respecting you.
Petruchio.	To her, Kate!
Hortensio.	To her, widow!
Petruchio.	A hundred marks, my Kate does put her down.
Hortensio.	That's my office.
Petruchio.	Spoke like an officer. Ha to thee, lad.

[Drinks to Hortensio]

Baptista.	How likes Gremio these quick-witted folks?
Gremio.	Believe me, sir, they butt together well.
Bianca.	Head and butt! An hasty-witted body
	Would say your head and butt were ahead and horn.
Vincentio.	Ay, mistress bride, hath that awakened you?
Bianca.	Ay, but not frighted me; therefore I'll sleep again.
Petruchio.	Nay, that you shall not. Since you have begun,
	Have at you for a bitter jest or two.

Bianca.	Am I your bird? I mean to shift my bush,
	And then pursue me as you draw your bow.
	You are welcome all.

[Exit Bianca with Kate and Widow]

Petruchio.	She hath prevented me. Here, Signior Tranio,
	This bird you aimed at, though you hit her not;
	Therefore a health to all that shot and missed.
Tranio.	O sir, Lucentio slipped me, like his greyhound,
	Which runs himself and catches for his master.
Petruchio.	A good swift simile but something currish.
Tranio.	'Tis well, sir, that you hunted for yourself;
	'Tis thought your deer does hold you at a bay.
Baptista.	O, O, Petruchio, Tranio hits you now.
Lucentio.	I thank thee for that gird, good Tranio.
Hortensio.	Confess, confess, hath he not hit you here?
Petruchio.	'A has a little galled me, I confess,
	And as the jest did glance away from me,
	'Tis ten to one it maimed you two outright.

Baptista.	Now, in good sadness, son Petruchio,
	I think thou hast the veriest shrew of all.
Petruchio.	Well, I say no. And therefore, for assurance,
	Let's each one send unto his wife,
	And he whose wife is most obedient
	To come at first when he doth send for her
	Shall win the wager which we will propose.
Hortensio.	Content. What's the wager.
Lucentio.	Twenty crowns.
Petruchio.	Twenty crowns!
	I'll venture so much of my hawk or hound,
	But twenty times so much upon my wife.
Lucentio.	A hundred then.
Hortensio.	Content.
Petruchio.	A match, 'tis done.
Hortensio.	Who shall begin?
Lucentio.	That will I.
	Go Biondello, bid your mistress come to me.
Biondello.	I go
	[*Exit*]

Baptista.	Son, I'll be your half, Bianca comes.
Lucentio.	I'll have no halves; I'll bear it all myself.

[Enter Biondello]

How now, what news?

Biondello.	Sir, my mistress sends you word

That she is busy and she cannot come.

Petruchio.	How? She's busy and she cannot come?

Is that an answer?

Gremio.	Ay, and a kind one too.

Pray God, sir, your wife send you not a worse.

Petruchio.	I hope, better.
Hortensio.	Sirrah Biondello, go and entreat my wife

To come to me forthwith.

[Exit Biondello]

Petruchio.	O ho, entreat her!

Nay, then she must needs come.

Hortensio.   I am afraid, sir,

Do what you can, yours will not be entreated.

    [Enter Biondello]

Now where's my wife?

Biondello. She says you have some goodly jest in hand.

She will not come. She bids you come to her.

Petruchio. Worse and worse. She will not come. O vile,

Intolerable, not to be endured!

Sirrah Grumio, go to your mistress; say

I command her come to me.

    [Exit Grumio]

Hortensio. I know her answer.

Petruchio.   What?

Hortensio.   She will not.

Petruchio. The fouler fortune mine, and there an end.

    [Enter Kate]

Baptista. Now, by my holidame, here comes Katherina.

Kate. What is your will, sir, that you send for me?

Petruchio. Where is your sister and Hortensio's wife?

Kate.	They sit conferring by the parlor fire.
Petruchio.	Go fetch them hither. If they deny to come,
	Swinge me them soundly forth unto their husbands.
	Away, I say, and bring them hither straight.
	[*Exit Kate*]
Lucentio.	Here is a wonder, if you talk of a wonder.
Hortensio.	And so it is. I wonder what it bodes.
Petruchio.	Marry, peace it bodes, and love, and quiet life,
	An awful rule and right supremacy;
	And, to be short, what not that's sweet and happy.
Baptista.	Now fair befall thee, good Petruchio.
	The wager thou hast won, and I will add
	Unto their losses twenty thousand crowns,
	Another dowry to another daughter,
	For she is changed as she had never been.

Petruchio.   Nay, I will win my wager better yet
             And show more sign of her obedience,
             Her new-built virtue and obedience.
                  [Enter Kate, Bianca, and Widow]
             See where she comes and brings your froward wives
             As prisoners to her womanly persuasion.
             Katherine, that cap of yours becomes you not.
             Off with that bauble, throw it under foot.
                  [She throws it]
Widow.   Lord, let me never have a cause to high
             Till I be brought to such a silly pass.
Bianca.   Fie, what a foolish—duty call you this?
Lucentio.   I would your duty were as foolish too.
             The wisdom of your duty, fair Bianca,
             Hath cost me five hundred crowns since suppertime.
Bianca.   The more fool you for laying on my duty.

Petruchio.	Katherine, I charge thee, tell these headstrong women
	What duty they do owe their lords and husbands.
Widow.	Come, come, you're mocking. We will have no telling.
Petruchio.	Come on, I say, and first begin with her.
Widow.	She shall not.
Petruchio.	I say she shall—and first begin with her.
Kate.	Fie, fie, unknit that threatening unkind brow
	And dart not scornful glances from those eyes
	To wound thy lord, thy king, thy governor.
	It blots thy beauty as frosts do bite the meads,
	Confounds thy fame as whirlwinds shake fair buds,
	And in no sense is meet or amiable.
	A woman moved is like a fountain troubled,
	Muddy, ill-seeming, thick, bereft of beauty,
	And while it is so, none so dry or thirsty
	Will deign to sip or touch one drop of it.
	Thy husband is thy lord, thy life, thy keeper,
	Thy head, thy soverign—one that cares for thee,

And for thy maintenance commits his body
To painful labor both by sea and land,
To watch the night in storms, the day in cold,
Whilst thou li'st warm at home, secure and safe;
And craves no other tribute at thy hands
But love, fair looks, and true obedience:
Too little payment for so great a debt.
Such duty as the subject owes the prince,
Even such a woman oweth to her husband,
And when she is froward, peevish, sullen, sour,
And not obedient to his honest will,
What is she but a foul contending rebel
And graceless traitor to her loving lord?
I am ashamed that women are so simple
To offer war where they should kneel for peace,
Or seek for rule, supremacy, and sway,
When they are bound to serve, love, and obey.
Why are our bodies soft and weak and smooth,
Unapt to toil and trouble in the world,
But that our soft conditions and our hearts

Should well agree with our external parts?
Come, come, you froward and unable worms,
My mind hath been as big as one of yours,
My heart as great, my reason haply more,
To bandy word for word and frown for frown.
But now I see our lances are but straws,
Our strength as weak, our weakness past compare,
That seeming to be most which we indeed least are.
Then vail your stomachs, for it is no boot,
And place your hands below your husband's foot,
In token of which duty, if he please,
My hand is ready, may it do him ease.

Petruchio. Why, there's a wench! Come on and kiss me, Kate.
Lucentio. Well, go thy ways, old lad, for thou shalt ha't.
Vincentio. 'Tis a good hearing when children are toward.
Lucentio. But a harsh hearing when women are froward.

Petruchio.   Come, Kate, we'll to bed.

We three are married, but you two are sped.

'Twas I won the wager [*To Lucentio*] though you hit the white,

And, being a winner, God give you good night.

  [*Exit Petruchio with Kate*]

Hortensio.   Now, go thy ways; thou hast tamed a curst shrow.

Lucentio.   'Tis a wonder, by your leave, she will be tamèd so.

  [*Exeunt*]

FINIS

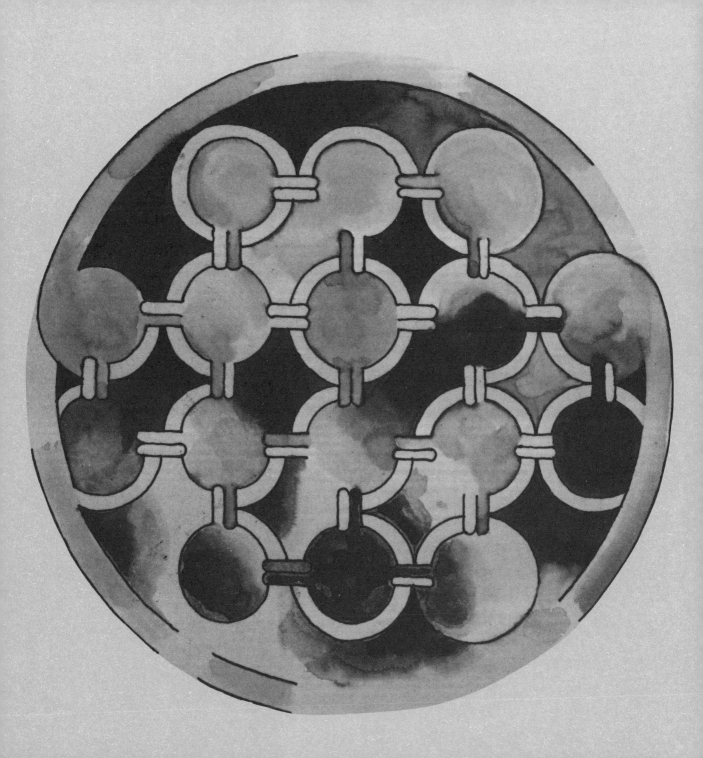

COLOPHON

Typography by the ComposingRoom inc.
The text was set in 14 pt. Kentonnian, 6 pt. leaded
with 12 pt. Italics. The display copy is Forum No. 274.
Complete page negatives were prepared for platemaking.
Printed Lithography by Thompson Lithographic Associates Inc.
on a 60-inch Harris 2-color press. The printing plates used were
custom ball grain aluminum wipe-on plates.
The paper manufactured by Finch, Pruyn & Company, Inc. is
Finch Textbook Offset, Vellum Finish, Cream White,
Basis 80, 312 pages per inch.
Bound with three-piece Holliston Cloth, Dull Black
Levant 7X back, and Kingston Natural 3555.
Endpapers are Elephant Hide, Sea Foam No. 23.
Illustrations are by Isadore Seltzer.
Design by Daniel Haberman.

WILLIAM SHAKESPEARE:
THE TAMING OF THE SHREW